Praise for **Notes to Boys**

One of *The Hairpin's* 15 books to read now
A *Hello Giggles* Item of the Day

"…what makes the book so good is that grown-up Pam has enormous affection for Little Pam, who is, like a little sister, horribly embarrassing on the one hand and a fiercely protected loved one on the other. It's a collection of embarrassing stories and mortifying notes, yes, but it's also a pretty deeply felt memoir about her introduction to boys and sex and, perhaps most painfully, learning when not to tell people how you feel."
—**Linda Holmes**, NPR's *Monkey See* and *Pop Culture Happy Hour*

"…I enjoyed the book, and I rooted for [Little Pam]…hang around for the payoff."
—Tiffany Turpin Johnson, *LitReactor*

Praise for **Pamela Ribon**

"Ribon's steadfastness in this character's lack of likability is admirable. She never panders by making Smidge somehow have some kind of epiphany of character simply because she is dying. Ribon is unwavering in what she shows us of Smidge and the novel is the better for it."
—Roxane Gay, author of *Hunger* and *Bad Feminist*

"…a book with all the elements I love: best friends, 'found' families, Ribon's trademark humor and vivid writing. (The description of Smidge's cancerous cough is heart-stopping.)"
—Jennifer Weiner, author of *Good In Bed* and *Who Do You Love*

"Hilarity and heartbreak compete, but ultimately hope wins in this thoroughly delightful story about what it means to be a woman, a mother, a best friend. I can't wait to pass this book along to every woman who ever mattered to me. Pamela Ribon has a huge, fresh voice, and this is her best book yet."
—Joshilyn Jackson, *New York Times* bestselling author of
Gods in Alabama and *A Grown-Up Kind of Pretty*

Notes to Boys

(And Other
Things I
Shouldn't
Share in
Public)

Also by Pamela Ribon

Slam!

You Take It From Here

Going In Circles

Why Moms are Weird

Why Girls are Weird

Notes to Boys

to

Boys

(And Other Things I Shouldn't Share in Public)

PAMELA RIBON

THIS IS A GENUINE RARE BIRD BOOK

A Rare Bird Book | Rare Bird Books
453 South Spring Street, Suite 302
Los Angeles, CA 90013
rarebirdbooks.com

Set in Minion
Printed in the United States

10 9 8 7 6 5 4 3 2 1

Paperback ISBN: 9781942600879

Publisher's Cataloging-in-Publication data

Ribon, Pamela.
Notes to boys (and other things I shouldn't share in public) : a mortifying
memoir / by Pamela Ribon.
p. cm.
ISBN 978-1940207056

1. Ribon, Pamela. 2. Ribon, Pamela—Humor. 3. First loves. 4. High school
girls—Biography. 5. High school students—United States—Biography. 6.
Adolescence—Anecdotes. I. Title.

CT275 .R528 2014
305.235/092—dc23

For my daughter.
May she love with all her heart.

And for my husband.
He's gonna keep her heart protected.
With, like, a secret knife.
And a big dog.

"I want to be with you now, right NOW, right NOW, right NOW, right now, now, now, now."
—Edie Brickell & New Bohemians, "Now"

"I know someday you'll have a beautiful life, I know you'll be the sun…in somebody else's sky, but why-hyy, whyyyyhyyy, WHYYYYY-HYYYY AH-Can't it be, ah-Can't it beeeeEEEeeeEEeeeEEEE MIIIIIIIIIIIIIIIAAAAAIAAAAAIIIIIIII-AHHHIIGH-HINE?!"
—Pearl Jam, "Black"

Introduction

Let's start with one of my first ridiculous moments in love: the night I forced my crush to watch *Broadcast News* with me.

I suppose technically he watched it while I watched him watching it—my eyes wide and mouth ready for the kiss I knew he'd give me as soon as he figured out that I was Albert Brooks and he...he...was my Holly Hunter.

This is where I should probably tell you that I was thirteen years old.

Needless to say, he didn't catch the subtext. During the moment when Albert Brooks tells Holly Hunter he wishes she were two people—"So I could call up the one who's my friend and tell her about the one I love so much."—my young soul mate spooned cookies and cream ice cream into the crook of his bare knee and remarked, "Heh-heh. If I spread my leg apart like this it looks like a butt with poops."

But my heart knew we were destined to be. Even the chance to watch this romantic comedy together was a miracle that I assumed was part of our destiny—I had just moved away, several states over, to a small, rural town in Texas, and for reasons I'll never understand, both of our parents allowed this visit. He flew to my house. On a plane. He arrived at baggage claim wearing a navy blue *Late Night with David Letterman* T-shirt. I know you don't need to know that, but you should know that I know that because it speaks to how important this was to me.

We only had a couple of days together—mere hours! This meant I needed him to make a move and make it soon if we were going to be young lovers running through the streets. So I took him to the most romantic place I knew. I took him to Six Flags.

I'd always wanted to be that tanned and sweaty girl in an endless line for a roller coaster. She's wearing a flimsy spaghetti-strap top and tiny shorts as she sits on the handrail that divides the lines into rigid sections. She's chewing gum, or maybe just letting it stretch across her tongue as she rests her dewy cheek against the strong, muscled shoulder of her boyfriend. I wanted one of those middle-distance staring, metal band T-shirt wearing, floppy-haired, unfortunate-skinned boyfriends. He's the one standing in the space between her parted knees. He's the one holding her weary body up as they wait for a thrill ride.

I craved that moment with a boy, our sweat-soaked love the only thing keeping us from sudden heatstroke.

But during our two-hour wait for a sixty-second coaster, my Holly Hunter only used the handrails to show me how he would skate them if he had his board. His only proclamations of love were to say, "For the love of fucking shit, why is Texas as hot as the surface of the sun?"

On his last night in my house, I got desperate. Assuming he needed the ultimate hint, I snuck into the room where he was sleeping, climbed on top of him, yanked off my shirt and put his hands on my bare chest. "I have a girlfriend," he blurted, not without a touch of fear in his voice. "She goes to another school."

Why was I the only pre-teen ready for a serious, adult relationship? When would someone want to talk with me at a coffee shop about Salinger and *Kids in the Hall* sketches? When would I find my true Holly Hunter?

The real tragedy is that nobody ever pulled me aside to gently inform me that some feelings I should keep inside, that not everybody deserves my truth. Or at least so much of my truth. Instead, I was all alone and determined to find the one boy who wanted all of it, all of me, who loved my words first, my body second.

Wait.

My words first, my brain second, my bookshelves third, and then my body.

No—my mixtapes! Then my body.

At some point someone should have said to me, "Hey. You kind of have a weird idea of how love goes that seems completely based on things you've watched on television. True love isn't just like that time on *Laverne & Shirley* when Carmine and some other guy were fighting over Shirley and they got into a fist fight and Shirley tried to break it up when Carmine accidentally punched her in the face. I don't know why you think that's what love feels like, but listen: that's fucked up."

Now that you can imagine the type of girl I was as I entered my very heady, super hormonal teen years, you should also know that I had a lot of time on my hands and access to a whole lot of paper. This was before the Internet (I would normally add a "thankfully" here, but since I'm not just uploading the contents of what I wrote, I'm going the extra step to publishing them, I have no reason to be grateful for anything, and nobody to blame but myself), so there was nothing to stop me that probably keeps other teens in check these days (i.e. bullying, public mockery). I spent many, many, way too many years writing love letters, poems, stories. I wrote obsessively. Compulsively. Constantly. And for the most part, I delivered those pages straight to their intended target.

But not before I saved myself a copy.

It's likely I kept the first drafts and hand delivered the more refined, less scribbly revision. All I know is I have boxes of notebooks and folders filled with evidence that I spent the majority of my teen years being an accidental stalker.

This is where you probably ask, *But why do you still have all those boxes of notebooks and folders?* It's a valid question. The only answer I can give you is, it's not hoarding if it's research.

I gift that statement to the other human magpies in the world, the ones who can't bear to toss things that hold even the slightest sentimental value. As someone who has three large bowls filled with wine corks, I understand. For those of you who still have boxes stuffed with high school theatre T-shirts or every issue of *Sassy* magazine, I carry your heart. I carry your heart in my heart. And I put that heart in a drawer with a whole lot of other hearts and some keychains with bank logos on them and some photo booth strips I keep planning on framing one day in a cute way and an Altoids tin of three-hole punch brads because I have a compulsion to save that's fueled by the fear of becoming meaningless.

While most of you would probably not find it wise to publish your teenage diaries, it is an effective way to get people off your ass for saving all your shit, along with the bonus of a possible tax deduction once you reach Hoarding Level 3, also known as "I'd better rent a storage unit before I end up with a divorce."

The first time I shared these letters and stories with my husband, we were still only dating at the time. I opened my gigantic green folder of past love and began reading one of the letters to him in an embarrassed, *Gosh, remember when you used to be like this?* sort of way.

I was a few sentences in when he closed his eyes. "Please stop," he said, holding up his hand—palm out, as if he needed to shield his face from any further harm.

I was immediately sympathetic. "Oh. I'm sorry. Is it because I'm talking about past boyfriends? I get it. It's hard to think of me loving someone else?"

"No, that's not it," he said, eyes still shut, shaking his head. "I'm mortified for you."

There's a certain face people make when they hear these letters. I've read them aloud at enough book readings and shows to be familiar with the normal human reaction. Every face is a little bit different in its severity, but it's a clearly recognizable expression of horrified sympathy. The eyes squint, involuntarily, and the brow becomes rippled with angst. The mouth has two choices—either the lower lip drops, exposing the teeth in a way that, if the listener chose to speak, he would say something like: "Eeeech." Or the mouth retreats, pulling back inside itself, teeth biting down—probably to keep from yelling at me, "Why are you doing this to yourself?!"

After a book reading last year, a woman around my age approached me, smiling nervously. "I just wanted to thank you for sharing your teen diaries with us," she said. "It made me do something really important."

Assuming she began mentoring at a high school or signed up to be a foster parent, I felt a swell of pride. "That's great! What did you do?"

"I called my mom and told her to burn all my old diaries and journals. I told her where they were in the basement and I made sure she got rid of them. All of them. I couldn't bear to imagine anyone finding them one day, even after I was dead, and reading them. You made me realize just how terrifying it would be if anybody ever saw them."

I was still quite flattered.

Part One

(Getting Serious About Boys)

19 SEPT., 1990

That's how I dated all these letters and poems. Just a shitload of commas and dots, numbers tossed about here and there. It was around the same time I started intentionally pronouncing "schedule" with a "sh" sound at the beginning. I do not know why I thought I'd be just a little British. I knew not one British person. I'd never been anywhere near that side of the planet. To this day I still say "leisure," with the soft "e" sound—something that doesn't come up all that often now that I no longer spend weekends playing Trivial Pursuit with my parents. I believe they avoided the orange category simply to keep my intentional affect from driving them crazy.

"Why do you keep saying it like that?" they'd ask.

"That's how I've always said it," I'd lie for absolutely no reason. And then they'd ground me.

On 19 Sept., 1990 I preserved a short moment of my life in a yellow Mead notebook. I am almost positive this story did not get duplicated and handed to the person starring in this entry because of how it ends.

19 Sept., 1990

The rain pours outside my window and [**NAME OMITTED**] is all I think about.

Here are some running themes you will soon pick up from my teen years: rain, windows, thinking. I will use pseudonyms for all boys in these pages because even the ones who were dicks to me don't deserve this kind of public ridicule. I will wait to give this one his nickname. He will soon earn it.

My mind is stuck in the past—an hour and a half ago.

That is exactly how long it took for me to get off the school bus, walk into my house, eat something, maybe call someone who wasn't home yet, possibly do all my homework, and then grab my "writing." Maybe I called it a "journal," but I bet I called it my "writing," and I'd probably penciled this moment of reflection into my *shhhedule.*

All I can think of is the way I felt—I'm still blushing now. His touch was so soft, so caring.

This is the story of the time a boy touched me really high on my thigh.

It may not have been the most romantic of places or times,

He touched me on a school bus.

but my environment seemed to disappear the moment he twined his legs with mine and linked our little fingers.

He may have been actually pinning my hand down so I couldn't stop him, while simultaneously making sure my feet were positioned in a way that I couldn't kick in defense.

Fun fact: School Bus Boy didn't look at me when this was happening. We were on the bus, it was on the way home, apparently it was raining, and while everyone around us was yelling and goofing off, School Bus Boy decided to see just how far he could get his hand up my skirt without actually talking to me, looking at me, or being anything close to my boyfriend.

This did not stop me from trying to romanticize the moment once I was safely home and alone in my room.

My face runs red remembering the feeling of his fingers tracing on my thigh. A flowing, bubbly feeling is all over my body and I can't seem to get this dopey pre-pubescent grin off of my face.

What exactly is a "pre-pubescent grin"? Is that the face of an innocent child after getting groped on a bus? Perhaps "grin" isn't the right word there.

His body was warm, and he was smiling. But it was all so secretive. [**four lines in pencil which I have erased**] And the rain pours on.

I'm sure I could have gone on for as long as the rain were it not for the deep thoughts that immediately followed.

What is a soul, anyway?

Here we go.

I mean, it's a word used often, usually by poets or hopeless romantics who need a word to show the depth of their emotion. But what is a soul? Is it my feelings, my emotions? Is it my thoughts?

Who could I possibly be writing this to? Was it someone I was trying to impress? Was I planning on giving this to School Bus Boy? Or worse—was I writing to some version of me in the future?

Is it my desires? Is it my dreams? Is it a ball of fire deep inside that gives me the strength to go on living?

I'm a little embarrassed to see I followed all my questions above with these questions here. Every time I think I'm more mature and wiser than the girl of 19 September, I end up writing or doing something that proves I am not. One thing is for sure: back then I definitely thought I was fucking deep.

When I say that someone is invading my soul, then, what do I mean? I know how I feel. I feel like that person has a place. A place in my life, in my heart, in my soul, whatever you want to call it. I feel lifted when that person is around me. I feel happy. I feel free. I'm light-headed. It usually is called love, whatever that word means. Why does the English language have all these words for all these things that can't be defined?

That last sentence is a mind-buster, isn't it? Why do we define things that *cannot be defined*, you guys? I mean, look how casual I am, asking is that love, *whateverthatwordmeans*? [Then I do a little head jerk that flips my bangs to the side.]

We must take a break from the story of School Bus Boy here, because a couple of weeks later I became involved in a pretty serious relationship. Just like School Bus Boy, let's let him earn his name in the letter.

But first, this would be a good segue to explain why I cannot watch the show *Hoarders*, because while all of you sit back and judge and cluck and wretch, I am breathless with anxiety, clutching my throat, thinking, *How can they just throw out that entire box of old onesies without asking which five are the most important?! They don't even know why she saved them! There's a **reason!***

No matter how many waterproof bins I acquire from The Container Store for my things, the one priceless item I can't seem to stockpile is my dignity.

I Oct 1990

His smile. His hair. His weird, warped, twisted, beautiful personality. That's how he will always live on in my mind. Forever.

As much as I know he's right, I can't bring myself to face reality. It's over.

This boy and I dated for exactly thirty-six hours. I cannot remember if we even had a conversation about whether or not we were actually boyfriend/girlfriend, but I do remember him calling me to break up with me. If he had to call to break up with me, it implies at some point we "got together" through word (because definitely not in deed). I'm guessing I hung up the phone and immediately lunged for my notebook, in order to catch all of this fresh emotion.

> It's over. I keep telling myself this as I play our song over and over again—

U2's "With or Without You." NOT THAT IT MATTERS. Also: apparently he could, in fact, live without me. Immediately.

> —as I wallow in my disgusting self-pity. I replay everything in my mind and I know that I did nothing wrong, he did nothing wrong. We just learned too much and too little about each other too fast.

That sounds like I had sex with this boy. I did not. I don't think anything happened but, like, a kiss? Maybe? Honestly, mostly I remember holding hands and listening to U2. And then a phone call the next day where he dumped me, because we apparently had learned both too much AND too little about each other too fast. I'm sure that's a Bruce Springsteen song or something.

Thirty-Six Hours Boy was on the small side, with brown, floppy hair (floppy skater hair will be a thing with me that started with Holly Hunter Boy and will continue on through my Johnny Depp fixation *(1987-present)*) and a thick, twangy accent. His real first name is super Southern, the kind of name that normally belongs to a country music star. I think his parents were wealthy, maybe? I'm fading here because this is literally all I remember about him. I no longer remember his last name. But back then on 1 October, oh, how I remembered everything.

> He said he cared. He said he'd never mess behind my back. Well, he did keep his promise.

I like to picture I'm holding some kind of martini here, wrist bent, elbow tucked into my hip. *"Well, he did keep his promise."* So bitter already, having never traveled to a second or third base.

> And I kept mine. When he held my hand, I knew it was the start of something good—really good. Something real. Something that will last. Something…whole and massive and whirling and twisting and—

It's probably good that he broke up with me as quickly as he did. For his sake.

> —passionate and beautiful and wonderful and exhilerating [*sic*] and hilarious and weird and giddy and tingly and estatic [*sic*] and there. I mean really *there*. He kissed without force, held me without domination.

Um…it sounds like he really didn't want to kiss me, nor hold me. Maybe because it was the start of something "weird."

> He *liked* me. He liked *me*. He liked me. And for one miraculous weekend he was mine and I was his and we pledged eternal faithfulness and we laughed.

I bet that was the first time I thought of putting the emphasis on a different word through repetition and I bet I thought I invented that shit.

Did we laugh because of the pledge? Did he pledge to be faithful and then bust out laughing and I was all, "We are laughing together because LOVE IS SO ESTATIC!"?

> We held each other. We shared numerous feelings and emotions: romance, fright, disgust, humor and wonder.

More than half of the numerous things we "shared" sound like they weren't fun at all. I seem to have given this boy one really shitty weekend of virginal song-looping, super-tight hand-holding, and maybe, I don't know…scab-picking? I'm just trying to nail down the "disgust" part.

We knew each other—I thought. It felt so great having someone care about *me*, someone who picked me up when I fell—

Definitely scab-picking.

—someone who wanted to be by my side instead of expecting me to do it without question. Someone who treated me as an individual and as a thing of beauty. Someone with common interests. Someone with common goals. Someone whom I respected and respected me. God, has anyone else ever felt like this or am I the only one with these feelings?

Wow. Okay, that sounds like I've found someone very special there. I've learned a lot about this boy, so for God's sake, I hope I don't go and do something stupid now, like learning *too little*!

He said he was serious. Serious about us. He said it, I heard him.

"I heard him, Your Honor."

What possesses a boy to change his mind in the course of 24 hours?

Let me answer that one for you real quick like, Little Pam. YOU do. It is important to note that from here on out my handwriting goes batshit crazy.

He called me. Said he needed to talk. Said he thinks he's tied down. Said he wants to be free. BE FREE?! Said he didn't want to hurt me. Then he said the worst. The F-word. FRIEND! He said he liked me, but he didn't want a girlfriend at the time. He said it's going too fast for him—was it for me? And that he doesn't really know me—do I agree?

Seems like he let me down kind of easy, and even gave me a couple of ways that I could try to talk him into seeing me again for another day of finger-linking and Bono-singing. Not like my first boyfriend in the fifth grade, with whom I'd only had one conversation the entire time we were "going together," the one who broke up with me by having Matt Fakes tell me at recess that my boyfriend didn't think I was cute anymore and he wanted to go with somebody else. I didn't even change Matt Fakes' name right there because I'm that kind of emotionally scarred to this day.

Not that I hoard all of these memories.

That's the last I've spoken to him in 5 hours.

That's my favorite sentence of this entire letter.

My heart aches at the loss. Then I thought of his words, "I hardly know you."

Which I'm guessing he said with like, a *lot* of fear because I was *intense.*

I thought about this. What was his middle name? What was his favorite movie? What kinds of books does he read?

Jesus, I am a NERD.

When did he start to like me? Why is he a grade younger than I am when he's the same age?

Ha!

What's his favorite ice cream flavor?

"Gosh, I hope it's 'Book,' just like mine!!"

What classes does he take in school? What does he want to be when he grows up? When is his birthday? Is he a virgin?

Did I really know this person that I pledged eternally faithful to? If he didn't know me, why did he care? Why did he want me as a girlfriend one day and a good friend the next?

WHAT DID I DO?

WHAT CAN I DO?

Boys are weird.

Thirty-Six Hours Boy and I had something special, but I didn't realize how special until a couple of weeks later.

The story continues thusly:

(I only use "thusly" to impress the me of 19 September, who would have raised one eyebrow to acknowledge me before breaking into a pre-pubescent grin.)

One night my parents were out of town, and because I wasn't a girl with a healthy amount of self-esteem, nor was I convinced the people I was hanging out with actually considered me a friend, they were somehow suddenly all over at my house, even though they weren't allowed, and even though I didn't know half of them, which means I was probably right that they didn't consider me a friend. I believe they were all pretty respectful, as far as a bunch of teenagers sitting in a stranger's house can be. They mostly used my couches to goof off, talk about music, and drink vodka out of thermoses. It was like a punk rock tea party. I imagine they discussed important topics of the day like skipping a pep rally, or the new Jane's Addiction album, or if it was better to buy Doc Martens at the sporting goods and uniform store where it's cheaper than to drive an hour away to the punk-goth boutique in downtown Houston for the authenticity.

The reason I don't know what they actually discussed is because I was in my bedroom, where School Bus Boy was seeing just how far he could get with me now that we were in a non-moving object. In the dark, in my bed, both fully clothed. Shoes on.

I do think, though, if I have to be completely honest, that we were not the only ones in the room. I mean, I know this. I know there was someone else on the floor of my room when we started kissing, and I know this because the boy on the floor would one day be my boyfriend, and he told me about this awkward night when he thought he was hanging out with some people, only to hear them start smacking away. I only include this fun fact because I think there's a real dividing line to our make out sessions in life. As long as you don't care if someone else is in the room listening to your sloppy slurps and groans, I think you can safely say you are still firmly in your youth. (Congrats, polyamorous ones!)

Anyway, our accidental creeper didn't get too much of an earful, as I had to deliver some bad news to School Bus Boy, which I whispered as seductively as I could muster.

"You have to stop now because I'm on my period."

School Bus Boy abruptly stood up and left the room.

I later found him in the kitchen, where I asked the only question appropriate for the moment.

"Are you mad at me?"

He looked anywhere but in my direction, seemingly uncomfortable. I can't imagine why.

"No, I'm not mad," he said. He quickly squeezed my hand before walking away. I remember the hand squeeze not because it was a sweet, silent comment on how he could empathize with how rough it must be to be a teen girl, but rather because he would intentionally grow out his fingernails and then file them to a sharp, claw-like point. (While it is hard to figure out who you are when you're a thirteen-year-old girl, I can't imagine how much more difficult the same thing must sometimes be for a thirteen-year-old boy.) I remember the squeeze because his pinkie nail dug into my palm, and it hurt like a bitch.

Once School Bus Boy left the kitchen, I was immediately confronted by my ex-boyfriend, Thirty-Six Hours Boy. It had been a good two weeks since our whirlwind romance, so I knew the wounds were still fresh for both of us.

"Did you just make out with [School Bus Boy]?" he asked, his face unreadable because I didn't understand boys.

"I don't know," I answered, trying to sound both smug and aloof.

Thirty-Six Hours Boy shook his head. "You did, didn't you?"

"Does that upset you?" I asked in a most soap-operatic fashion. I might have placed my hand on a doorframe for optimum emotional leaning.

"Yeah," he said, pushing past me. "You made him win."

I spent the rest of the weekend mulling that over. *You made him win.* What cryptic message was my past true love telling me? Did he want me back? Were they both after my heart and it somehow seemed like I had made a choice? What had he won— the chance to own my heart?

I had days to figure it out, as I was super-grounded after that night. I got busted due to the traces my former lover Thirty-Six Hours Boy had left behind—the master bathroom toilet seat was raised. This means: BOYS WERE HERE AND YOU ARE GROUNDED.

I couldn't be bothered to spend my imprisonment thinking of what I'd done to anger my parents when I had to figure out what I'd done to upset Thirty-Six Hours Boy. He seemed so troubled.

You made him win.

Win what? I was unable to sleep, so firmly in the middle of such an emotional triangle. *Oh, boys! Gentlemen. Do let us try to be civil. Perhaps I should hear each of your desires listed in order of importance before I choose which of you shall next slide a hand near my underpants as we ride our bright yellow chariot. Please also list your top five favorite books and ice cream flavors. Thank you.*

In the lunchroom a few days later, there was a small commotion. At a table far from where I sat, two girls I did not know were yelling at each other. As it got heated, word was spreading. The girls were friends, good friends, and something had come between them. Their fight escalated, and they stormed out of the room together.

They returned soon after, making a beeline to School Bus Boy's table, where they stopped. A few words were exchanged before one of the girls slapped School Bus Boy across the face. Then the other girl slapped him, harder. The crowd shouted, "Oooh!" The girls left holding hands, and School Bus Boy stared at his lap.

This is when Thirty-Six Hours Boy stopped by my table. "They found out about the bet. Dumbass gave both of those girls the same apology letter, when he should have known they were best friends. What an idiot. But that's how he beat me, three girls to two."

Thirty-Six Hours Boy walked away. I never spoke to him again.

I still remember how hot my face got as I stared down at my lunch tray wondering, "*Why didn't I get a letter?*"

The Continuing Story
of Holly Hunter Boy

I skipped ahead to give you an idea of what kind of letters I wrote to boys, because I don't have too many pieces of evidence for what I did to Holly Hunter Boy, the one I forced to watch *Broadcast News* all those years ago. For him, I just threw everything at him, first draft, and let it ride.

But I need to go back because you should probably know I once wrote him a two hundred-page letter.

That takes a second to understand, I know. What I did was I bought a brand new, spiral notebook and I filled it over the course of a weekend. In pen. And maybe some colored pencils. Probably some highlighter. I feel like maybe the cover of the notebook was green. But inside those pages was pure, unfiltered, unedited angst.

At the time, I figured there was no clearer way to express my love in a way that kept me from having to actually say any words out loud. I could slide a note (or in this case, drop a thick-ass notebook) onto a desk, disappear around a corner, and let this boy have his *moment* with my head, my heart. I was convinced he would sit there and absorb how incredible this all is, how lucky we are to be two people in love like this. That's what I would do if someone treated me this way!

[Reality check: no, it isn't. When I one day received a twenty-page letter left for me on the windshield of my car, telling me all the ways I didn't understand how much I was supposed to belong to the author of that confession, I did not feel special. I did not feel loved. I felt stalked and a little like maybe I should find a new city in which to live. But the story of that boy is for later, as it's nowhere near this time, when I would have given anything for this level of attention.]

People mock the Manic Pixie Dream Girl now, but I think back then, before that cliché was invented, that's what I thought I was. That's what I wanted to be. Pixie part aside, that's really who I was: that sweet, innocent girl with one hand holding office supplies stuffed with love, the other handing over a mixtape that no doubt started with Metallica's "Fade to Black" and ended with "Pretty Little Ditty" by the Red Hot Chili Peppers.

Despite all I put Holly Hunter Boy through over the years when I was living in the same city, once I was hundreds of miles away, we became rather good friends. As we got older, old enough to have actual problems and things to do, we settled into a friendship that consisted of two phone calls a year, one for each of our birthdays. We are almost six months apart in age, so for the past twenty-five years or so, every early April and every late September, we call each other to catch up.

When we were younger our calls could be longer. We had time to chat about classes or people we were dating. We talked about parents, movies, and music. But as time got more precious, our phone calls became not just something we looked forward to, but a kind of quick progress report on our lives.

"You moved to Central America?"

"You're writing for a TV show?"

"I can't believe you have a doctorate!"

We've been there through each other's marriages and mortgages, divorces and deaths. If one of us can't talk on our actual birthdays, the reason has to be really good.

"Hi, I can't talk today. I'm in Hawaii and I'm running a marathon in the morning."

"Hi, I can't talk today. There's a hurricane headed toward my parents' house."

We've seen each other in person on only two occasions since the weekend of *Broadcast News*—once when we were in college, and once in our mid-twenties, before I moved much further away, to Los Angeles. There have been times when we didn't live too far apart, or when one of us was on a trip that took us closer to the other one, but as we got older, with the cats in the cradle and all, we just hadn't been able to schedule being in the same room together.

We don't even use Facetime or Skype. I think because we've always known each other better as a voice over the phone.

My husband is Southern—from the Gulf Coast—which is not all that far from Jackson, Mississippi, where I fell for Holly Hunter Boy. There are times my husband's talking when I hear the way he can make the word "on" sound like "*own*," and I recognize that late-night, talking-in-the-dark feeling of Holly Hunter Boy in my ear.

A text from me on his birthday in 2011: *Happy Birthday, mister. Shall we schedule phone time?*

His reply: *I didn't realize that we had an option. Call when you get up. I should be free. I'll make an outline of talking points before then. We have a lot to cover.*

Me: *Will charge the phone. Looking forward to it.*

The next year he didn't call on my birthday. That had never happened before. I didn't want to bother him, but I worried.

Three days later, he texted:

"*Sorry I didn't call for your birthday. I was kinda busy.*"

And then there's a photo of him leaning over a tiny baby, staring into a pair of huge, glassy eyes that peered back from just below that ubiquitous striped knit cap of the newly-born.

"*Best reason ever. Congrats, daddy.*"

"*Happy belated. I'd like to call soon.*"

What Holly Hunter Boy didn't know when he sent that photo was that six hours earlier I had learned I was pregnant.

Our lives have remained connected in that way, and if I had any good sense I would let it be this sweet thing that has just the right amount of nurturing. It's the kind of relationship I would want with someone if I didn't already have it. It's a nice resolution to all these heartbreaks and yearnings I put myself through over my high school years.

But then I started writing this book, and I got to thinking.

I sent a text to Holly Hunter Boy, telling him about the book, adding that it was a shame he didn't still have that two-hundred page letter, as I can't imagine what was in it. I was then like, *Maybe I could interview you or whatever, ha ha.*

He texted back: *What are you talking about? Of course I have the note. And I have always assumed any interaction was an interview. Will send as soon as I locate it.*

That was a couple of months ago. No package has arrived in the mail, but I've been assured it is coming.

I will now compartmentalize my anxiety about what will happen if I ever see that two-hundred page letter again by going back to when I was too self-absorbed to have any shame. Ladies and gents, I return you to: *the nineties.*

Share With Me Your Soul
(The Heartbreak of Homeroom Boy)

I'm just so in awe of how much passionate heartache I was capable of feeling all by myself.

8 Nov 1990

It doesn't matter what I try to do. Every time I try to do something you start to take control again. You creep into my soul—you've perfected it by now—and occupy my every thought, every move, every emotion.

What is this, five weeks after Thirty-Six Hours Boy? You guys, I'm talking about a completely different boy here. A COMPLETELY DIFFERENT HUMAN BEING. And if that's not enough, you should know that my only interaction with this boy is that we had homeroom together.

That is it. That is all. I saw him for an hour a day. He was also on the small side, with dark, curly hair and a shy sense of humor I found endearing. We were thrown together by fate: our last names were very close alphabetically.

You make my pulse race, my stomach jump, my eyes roll back in ecstacy [sic] as I think of the feeling of your body twined with mine and your voice filling my head, pounding, twirling, twisting and whirling until I want to scream.

That sounds *awful*. Again, it's important to note that in this case, as in many cases of my unsent letters…this boy has not only not ever kissed me, he most likely has no idea I even like him. Yet, I like him enough that I volunteer to have the experience of his voice whirling in my head until I scream.

Speaking of which, for the first half of the last sentence it sounds like I'm describing a key scene in *The Exorcist*.

But I can't.

Can't what? Can't scream? I don't understand why not.

I'm afraid. It hurts to say the truth. I can't tell you how my heart cries when you aren't near me.

Which means my heart was crying pretty much any minute of my life other than the forty-three minutes of homeroom. No wonder I wasn't participating in sports, you guys. My heart was weeping. How can I be expected to run laps when my aorta needs a Kleenex?

I can't tell you how my ears long for the sound of your voice.

"—because you don't pick up the phone when I call."
Actually, eventually we do spend long hours on the phone. I don't know how I tricked him into staying on the phone with me while we did homework and watched different things on television, but eventually I did just that.

I can't tell you how my mind yearns for your wit.

My mind *yearns*, okay? For *wit*.

And I sure can't tell you how much my body longs for your touch. Your kiss. Your breath from your whispers dancing on my neck.

I can't tell you because I have no idea how that feels or if I'd even want that because I'd probably freak out if you just huffed down the front of my shirt in order to make a whispery neck-dance.

> I need you. I want you. But I can't tell you. Why can't I tell you?

Because he keeps running away? If only I could catch him! Damn this weepy heart!

> You asked me if I knew what love is.

I feel like maybe he didn't. Or, if he did, his question was either sarcastic or rhetorical. Perhaps both. The point is: never ask a fifteen-year-old girl if she knows what love is. Well, don't ask fifteen-year-old me. It appears to cause some problems.

Know that I want to interrupt every sentence that's coming up in this next little batch, but I think I should just let it all come out at once here, like a Band-Aid that was taping up this teenage mortification gash.

> I don't know, is this feeling love? Oh, no, it can't. Love is supposed to be this amazing, glorious feeling and all I feel is pain. Agony. Torture. I feel it when you are gone. I feel it when you are near. Because all I can think of is how much I want to take you and hold you close forever.

Three years later, Sarah McLachlan will compose a hit song using only these words.

> But I can't. Not yet. Not until I know you love me too. Do you?

"Well, I—"

Wait, do I love you? Is this love?

"—Oh, I should go."

Is it love when you always want to be by that person's side? Or maybe love is measured on how much you know about a person.

Uh, I thought we already covered this five weeks ago!

Do I know you? Oh, but I do. I know your smile, your laugh, your humor. I know your name, your family, your house.

"Your house." I'm pretty sure I meant it in the Shakespearean way. "*I pledge thee my love, Homeroom Boy, you who are the greatest of the Homeroom Houses.*"

I really did strike out those words in the letter, as if I couldn't live with lies in a letter nobody was ever going to see but me. I am sure I agonized over striking out the words, which is probably why I didn't scribble over them until they were illegible, but rather drew a single, solitary, sad line. It must have killed me to do so. Because the truth is, I didn't know his full name. Only first and last, not middle.

And you guys, remember: knowing someone's full name is important when determining whether or not you have enough information to determine whether or not you love them.

I like how I started with these driver's license facts, "Well, I know where you live and I'm practically a member of your family." And then I was like, "Except I don't know where you live and I've never met anyone related to you, but I do know your *humor*, so we are soul mates. Now get in my arms so I can commence holding you FOREVER."

Again, please remember: the only relationship I have with this boy is that we do our homework together over the phone.

…*You* know what I mean. We work on *declensions*. Every night! Awwwwww, *yeah*!

This next passage is absolutely humiliating.

I know what you do during the day because I talk to you all night. I know how you think. I know how you work. I know how you feel. I know what you like to do.

I know what you don't. I know what you love. I know what you hate. The only thing that I don't know is the feeling of your lips against mine or the touch of your hands or heart. And for that sensation I would *kill*. Is that love?

NO. No, it is not.

Actually being able to kill, steal, lie, *die* for a person. Oh, God I'm in *love*. With you.

If love is the end-all, be-all feeling, why do I feel so horrible?

And the letter just ends here, like I threw down my journal and wandered off into the woods, searching for an answer, or perhaps to go kill someone, steal a wallet, and then die.

I don't know how many of you out there reading this happen to be fifteen. But if you are and somehow you're unlucky enough to be like, even a third as dorky as I was, please know that it gets better. Life does get better. Just not for, like, a bajillion years. And I know it's SO NOT FUNNY right now, how you feel, and everybody who laughs at you can just go suck it. In about ten years you'll find these letters and it still won't be funny, and then in, like, fifteen years you'll find them again and someone will laugh and you will be like GET OUT OF MY ROOM, but right around the twenty year mark you might see a couple of these letters and think, *Wow. Okay, maybe that one went a little too far.*

(But P.S.—I know, it's still not all that funny because your feelings are real and true and deserve to be validated and you deserve to be heard. You are a good person, and boys can be so mean.)

Where Are You Going, Homeroom Boy?

The next two letters are written in red pen. That can't be a good sign.

13, Nov., 1990

Why are you doing this to me?

It is all your fault, you know. You have to be so damn beautiful. So damn perfect in any way. You made me fall in love with you. You knew what you were doing from the beginning, didn't you? Don't flash those innocent brown eyes at me, I know how well you manipulate.

I wonder if I imagined this boy reading this letter and being flattered by it. Because the weird coy hostility here isn't working at all. Little Pam's got *no game*.

I need to refer to this version of myself as "Little Pam" to keep a bit of distance between me and the girl who wrote…well, this:

You've brainwashed me, that's it.

I'm sure when I finished writing this—and oh, believe me when I say it's a first draft and there are almost *zero* corrections (I'll be sure to let you know whenever I changed my mind mid-genius)—as *soon* as I finished the last loopy scribble, I know I flipped back to the first page and read the entire thing out loud. Even then I knew that if it didn't sound right, it didn't read right.

I'm wondering how I performed this one. I bet I was *so creepy*, reading it with what I assumed was a sexy smirk. I'm not one to advocate teenage sex or any kind of adult behavior among the little, but maybe if by fifteen I had at least an *idea* of what sex or sexiness was that wasn't solely acquired by watching Cinemax in the middle of the night I'd have made, like thirty-two percent less of a fool of myself. *Maybe.* Maybe twelve percent.

But back to the cheeky sex kitten known as Little Pam. I believe she was blushingly accusing her beloved of the amorous act of brainwashing.

> There's just no other explanation. It's brainwashing when that person something monopolizes your every thought, every move, every wish, every desire, every command, every motion, every breath, every tear, every smile, every sight, every sound, every laugh, every second of every minute of every hour—

Yeah. Yeah, I did. Wrote it all out. Because you know what's hot? Nouns and units of measurement.

> —of every day of every week of every month of every year, every dream, every nightmare, every sigh, every movement, every feeling, every word you say or write, and being helpless and completely out-of-control.

That sentence went all crazy at the end, didn't it? I mean, I know it was crazy throughout. I KNOW that, okay? I'm just saying, I had to go back through the list to figure out how I wrote myself out of that one.

But forgive LP her meandering sentence structure. I mean, can you imagine how hard it must have been? Having her sighs brainwashed?

> I know you caused this. Because you are the object of these feelings, thoughts and desires. You are what makes my sun rise and set. You are what brightens my day and makes it darken again. You are what brings

me joy and pain. You are what causes confusion and understanding.

YOU CAUSE ME UNDERSTANDING.

You are what causes laughter and tears. You are what causes hope and utter helplessness, you are what causes sleepless nights and stressful days. You are what makes my life liveable [*sic*]. But if you make my life suck so much, then why do I just keep on loving you?

It's *really* hard to be fifteen.

Because you are making me, that's why. Because you know that you have me at your beck and call and that you've got me drooling on your shoes in a disgusting religious sacrifice show of affection.

Please don't make me comment any further on that one. I... you know what's funny? AND I'M NEVER GOING TO DO THIS, but part of me wants to find this person and apologize but it would end up being on Facebook because I've seen him on Facebook, but then I'd be WRITING HIM A LETTER. AGAIN.

You know I'd do anything for you: lie, cheat, steal, kill, *die*, and that's just what makes you happy. Go ahead. Fuck with my head.

Oooohhh. Someone got out her Nine Inch Nails album.

Make me miserable. Make me cry. Make me scream in agony and weep in misery. Make me whimper. Make me sigh. I'll still love you. But you knew that, right?

And again, it just ends there because apparently I threw my journal across the room and then ran into the kitchen to drown my sorrows in a bowl of potato chips and a glass of whole milk. What? My parents both worked, okay? They didn't have time to teach nutrition! If they were home and available to talk to me and feed me carrots and celery, do you have any idea how hard it would have been for me to become a comedy writer? It would have been nearly impossible. I mean, as a woman.

Unrequited love, one spiral-bound notebook and a refrigerator filled with high-calorie snacks. THIS is how you make a success!

Anyway, I guess I ate all that, then ran back into my room, slammed myself down on my daybed, draped my so-cool black-and-white striped comforter over my shoulders, and…wrote some more.

13, Nov., 1990

It's *not* fair. It's *not* fair. I never did anything to you.

I am so sure that's untrue. I mean, even if we don't count the apparent stalking, I feel like I must have done something to make this kid be totally weirded out by me.

Actually, if this was written before I'd actually spoken to Homeroom Boy, then I'm just stating some facts. I've done nothing to him. His only crime so far was being seated near me, which is really more something one should blame on the alphabet.

I never did anything mean or rotten to mess with your mind. I never teased you or hurt you. I've never been anything but nice to you. So why do you keep torturing me? Why must I sit in agony day after day after day? If we are such great friends, and I'm supposed to be able to tell you anything and everything, and you are supposed to be able to tell me anything and everything, then how come I can't bring myself to tell you how I feel about you?

So it appears I have spoken to Homeroom Boy and I am living inside the Friend Zone. If you asked him, I doubt the terms of our relationship included me telling him "anything and everything," but to me he didn't have to ask.

And you aren't helping matters much keeping to yourself like that.

That might just mean "living at his own house" but I'm going to guess it means "asking me to please turn around and face forward in my chair."

What are you thinking? What's going on inside your mind? Is it anything like the anguish I feel knowing that your lips are only a foot away from mine, and yet they can't break each other's barriers because of a bond called friendship?

I'm guessing he's thankful every day for that barrier. I bet he's thankful every second of every minute of every hour of every day of every month of every year.

Are you confused too? Do you stay up at nights, wondering if we'll ever be together? Do you love me? Do you need me? Do you want me? Do you even like me?

Oh, that last one's so sad, isn't it? I'm haggling down to like.

If you've never done any of these things or asked yourself the same questions, then your hell doesn't even compare to the hell you are putting me through. Do you have any idea what it's like to live day to day just to see someone's face? Or hear someone's voice? You are all I live for. You are everything. You are my heart and my soul and my mind. I need you. I want you. I love you. If you need me, I'm here. If you want me, I'm here.

"In my room. Because I'm totally grounded for talking on the phone after nine on a school night."

If you love me, I'm yours. Take all of me. I will enter a state of bliss that might only compare to the ecstacy [sic] of heaven.

Probably I don't have to tell you this, but it's going to be another few years from this point before I lose my virginity.

> But if you don't want me, just say so. Please, my heart can't take much more. If you want me to go, I'll gather my sorrows and exit your life forever, although I don't know how I'll survive without you.

I like how I won't even finish the sentence that gives him the option to tell me to go without the threat of my immediate death on his hands. I only need time enough to gather my sorrows.

> I won't survive. Survival is painful without love.

Indeed, LP. Indeed.

> Survival is painful with love, if the object of your desire is keeping his feelings a secret. Won't you tell me? Share with me your soul.

If someone's keeping a list somewhere, this sentence is my new number one for Most Embarrassing.

> Please. I want to hear you, feel your words dancing in my mind and tickling my ears. Oh, heavenly bliss! I need to feel your body twined with mine. I want to stare into your eyes and be swept into another dimension.

Oh God, I think I'm in love. Now I'm scared.

And then it just ends here like I threw my journal across the room, ripped off all of my clothes and ran around my backyard in a frenzy fit for *The Bacchae*.

Good God, that thing was filled with so many hormones I think I just caught a zit. What a horrible day I had on 13, ,.Nov.,.. 199,0. Why won't that boy sweep me into another dimension with his chocolate-brown eyes and tell me if he even likes me? Why is he torturing me so, just going to class and then going home and then going to class again? Doesn't he understand my body needs twining?

The thing is I had *friends* back then. I guess I didn't tell any of them any of this? I don't think I did. Thank goodness I eventually got into theatre, so that I didn't have so much time to lock myself in my room while not doing a very good job of babysitting my little sister back when every day felt like a million days all squished into one sad, horrible, never-ending day. You know what never made it better? A bowl of Charles Chips and a glass of whole milk. But I tried. Every day. Until I was gi-normous.

20, Nov., 1990

> You must really hate me. You do, don't you? Jesus, did I smother you or something? What did I do to completely change your mind about me? Was it something I said? Something I did? Oh, if only I could journey through your mind and probe your inner thoughts.

Yeah, that's some sentence, right there. I wish I could tell you what prompted this letter, but I don't remember. Let's see, it's been a week since the last angry letters, so in this case I'm guessing he's taken to avoiding me? I mean, if he's smart, that's what he's doing. I truly don't remember.

> Do you hear me? I love you, dammit. I need you. My survival depends on it. Now I have the next four days all to myself, left completely alone.

Yikes, I hope I have enough paper to handle the next four days. Oh, look at the date—it must be Thanksgiving weekend. It's only the SADDEST WEEKEND EVER for a teen in love with Homeroom Boy! Already converting all those seconds and minutes into hours and days! How can I possibly be thankful when they haven't invented a machine that allows me to probe inner thoughts?!

Completely lost. Completely confused. Completely empty. I want to cry, but I can't. I want to scream, but I can't.

The screaming, again. I guess I can't scream because I'll get in trouble? That must be it. I don't know why I can't cry, other than possibly I'm starting to realize maybe I'm not as emotional over this boy as I think I should be.

I want to run to you, but I can't.

Because you won't tell me where you live and we have this four-day weekend that you want to spend with your *family* instead of your soul mate, you selfish, cocoa-eyed boy.

I just have to sit here on my ass and wonder what went wrong. I want to show my feelings, but I'm so empty that I can't even cry. Not that anyone would listen. The only one who ever really listened to me was you. And I can't very well tell you about how much I needed you.

And then it just ends here like I threw my journal aside and shoved my face into my pillow and made crying sounds but not one tear.

20 November ends up being kind of a banner day in this one-woman romance. It sounds like maybe Homeroom Boy used the very last second before a four-day weekend to say, "*Happy Thanksgiving. Hey, also, if you could just leave me alone forever that would be great. Bye.*"

I have to say I'm pretty impressed with Homeroom Boy on that one. Way to handle LP.

20, Nov., 1990

So this is heartbreak. So this is heartache. So this is what it feels like to be scum.

I have to guess that the only thing that went on between the writing of the last letter and this one is an unanswered phone call, or one where his mom or sister said, "Hold on...*Huh? You don't—Oh.* Um, he's not here right now, can I take a message?"

> It's even more painful than love. And I thought that love sucked. Love was a giggle compared to this.

That's fucking poetry, man. Something I should probably note here is that this isn't written on spiral paper. It's on loose-leaf three-punch lined paper, which means I was probably planning on handing him this letter.

> I feel so empty. I feel so alone. Why did you do this to me? You said it was too fast.

Oh, shit. I guess I DID get friend-dumped. You guys, friend-dumping. It's so sad. I'm so sad for LP. She's so confused. How did she get friending so *wrong*?

> Too fast? How? We've known each other a year and a half and you've never even held my hand. You've never kissed me. You've never held me. You've never told me you loved me. Now all of a sudden you need me to leave you alone?

It appears I had been given an order! I am sure it was clear and direct. "Leave me alone." I bet I won't listen!

P.S.: If I'd been told by an authority figure to do something, I completely would have listened, as "Getting In Trouble" was—and still is—the worst thing that could ever happen to me. But since this is just a boy who doesn't understand how important it is that I love him, I will continue to make sure he is really sure that he means "Leave me alone." I mean, first of all, there's so many ways to interpret what he's saying. And really, if you look at it, it's only three words, what he said. I've said WAY more words than that. So, you know. I'm clearly better at this than he is.

> What did I do? I just want you back. I need you. Maybe you'll feel this emptiyness emptyness [*sic*] as well. Maybe you'll miss me. Maybe you'll know how it feels

to have your heart torn from you. What do you mean "It's not gonna happen."?

One guess, little me.

It's so final. So serious. So fucking painful. Don't you like me anymore? How come you did five days ago? Enough to discuss it with the others.

The others! I can't believe I don't have any letters from five days previous, when I found out somehow that he liked me maybe kind of. Where are the happy letters? Wait. I bet I wrote them and gave them to him and then he called me to say, "IT'S NOT GONNA HAPPEN. LEAVE ME ALONE."

But you know, again, I have to say…he's not really being all that clear. I mean, LP likes you to break it to her super-gently. Like, say over the course of five years.

Now you call me like nothing has happened. What's your deal? Do you love me or hate me? There are no in-betweens. No exceptions. Love doesn't make exceptions.

And it ends there because that's some powerful shit LP just laid down.

Okay, so let's see here. It appears I have a friend who is a boy who is getting all these love notes from me and said somehow, "We're just friends and only going to be friends." He might have even said, "Leave me alone." But I bet he was like, "Now who's going to do my homework over the phone?" and called me, hoping I'd have already gotten over him. So, you know, in my defense… that's pretty stupid, right?

Because, you guys, what happens next is so embarrassing that a friend of mine and I wrote an entire comedy show around it. I mean, our show was ultimately about other things entirely, but the inspiration was this one moment in my teen life where I made a pretty big mistake.

It starts with this.

20, Nov., 1990

Homeroom Boy—

I think I have a problem. Great tone to start a letter with, I know. But just please listen to me.

See, there's this guy, and I really think I fucked things up between him and me. See, we've been pretty good friends for a while, but lately we've gotten to know each other better.

You guys, can LP get a high-five for how super-casual she's pulling off this tone? It's like, "Hey, friend. Can we talk, FRIEND TO FRIEND? See, I've got this friend who's totally not you, so don't you worry. I just need some ADVICE. About this GUY. I'M LITTLE PAM AND I LOVE YOU."

I always thought he was cool, so there's never been anything real awkward between us.

I have no idea what that means.

I guess we hit it off right away.

But I do know that right there I am straight-up quoting a lyric from the "Cell Block Tango" from the musical *Chicago*, so that's awesome. You know who knew the lyrics to *Chicago* in 1990? Ann Reinking and me. That's it.

Now, don't get the wrong idea about him, [HOMEROOM BOY], he's always been a perfect gentleman. He's never been anything but nice to me, and everyone agrees that he's a great guy. My problem? I'm getting to it, just hold on.

I can't believe how embarrassing this still is.

I don't know how or why, but we started to become closer and closer. I thought that maybe I was forcing him or something, but he called me as often as I called him. He's different from most of the other guys. Most of the others are constantly making disgusting sexual comments or whatever to me, and commenting on the size of my chest, but like I said, he was different.

I'm not going to say anything here, but I'm sure you need a break, so…go ahead. Catch your breath.

And I don't know. Maybe. He might have been gay. I DON'T KNOW. We never talked about it. Because there was no such thing as gay at that school at that age. Gay wasn't invented in that part of Texas until at least 1992.

So, I found myself thinking about him more and more. He was, like, always on my mind. But I kept trying to make myself not like him. I kept telling myself that he was only a friend, and that's all he'd ever be, a great friend. Even [K] thought that I should leave it at friendship, because we were so close.

K was my best friend, and she must have known he didn't like-me like me and was trying to find a way to tell me without telling me, which you'd think I'd be so easy to faux-talk to, what with how telling someone without telling someone appears to be the entire point of this letter.

And I took all the advice, but…well, you know that little voice inside of you that constantly goes on about how you need someone, and how it goes on about this one person until you can't get that person out of your head? Well, that little voice started rambling about that guy. And while I forced my head to concentrate on my studies, my heart pulled up a chair to chat with the little fucker.

This is where I worry that my writing hasn't improved in the slightest since 20, November, 1990.

And my heart ate all of that sappy shit up and started fluttering and fainting whenever that person was around.

Fainting Heart Syndrome affects one out of every five dorks, and it's truly no laughing matter. Symptoms include: a weeping heart, confusion and understanding, a yearning for wit, hypergraphia, sighs that sound brainwashed, an inability to cry despite feeling overwhelming sorrow, an urge to kill and/or die for a near stranger, and a fixation on having someone's breath dancing upon one's virgin neck. A heart murmur is a giggle compared to Fainting Heart Syndrome.

I started feeling stupid. But I was kind of drawn to him, you know? I tried to keep my heart away from him, by being with other guys, but once my heart makes up its mind, the rest of my body is hopelessly helpless. It's actually quite a pitiful sight. I always talk about that person. I dream about him. I wish for him. And then, when I know I'm truly hooked, I write about him. Not dopey notes like the ones I give you. These are full-blown mushy sappy sexual romantic tear-jerking love letters.

Are they? I mean, really, is that what I thought they were? I'm not talking about now, when you and I are maybe crying over these things because of extreme mortification or PTSD flashbacks from various high-school heartbreaks. I mean did I think, back then, that a fifteen-year-old boy would read these letters and find himself actually moved to tears?

This also sounds like I'm threatening him. *"Mister, you think you're getting notes now, you should see the ones I haven't let you see. You will WEEP."*

Do I send them? Hell, no. No one has even seen them. You are the first I've told about them.

Anyway, I was writing pages and pages about the guy. I was in love, I thought. About this time, people began to bug me about him. Do I like him? Do I love him? Does he like me? Is he going to ask me out? Like I'm fucking Nostradamus or something.

I just so desperately wanted to be cool.

I couldn't very well ask him. I just kind of played it cool, you know. I didn't tell anyone my feelings, because my head was still trying to talk my heart out of this mess it was getting me into. Then I found out that he liked me. He told one of my friends who told me. So, I'm estatic [*sic*], right? And I'm ready to leap into his arms and be carried off into the hokey sunset.

LP's developing a cynical jaded streak right before our very eyes. This unrequited love, WHICH LASTED LESS THAN THREE WEEKS, is possibly to blame for a good third of my (possibly still current) trust issues. *Like I'm fucking Nostradamus*, indeed.

I would have done anything for him, [HOMEROOM BOY]. I still would. Lie, cheat, steal, beg, kill, *die*— nothing was too much. I began needing him more and more. I knew I was in love, and to tell you the truth, I was scared shitless, because I know that when I fall in love it's forever and I never fall out of love, only move on.

Pausing to let you know here that I just had to turn the page. Because we are now on PAGE FOUR.

I wasn't going to leave this guy. [HOMEROOM BOY], he was, well, is, so nice. He's a great guy, really. He's hilarious and good looking—great looking and all.

If I recall correctly, in the live show, this is when we put his yearbook picture up on the giant screen. I won't do it for you here, now, because lawsuit.

So now you're like, so? What's the deal? My deal is my problem:

He told me that he doesn't like me. Well, he didn't use those words, he kinda said it wasn't going to work out. He was real nice about it, I mean, I know he didn't mean to hurt me, but there's really no nice way to crush someone's heart. But I'm not blaming him or anything, it's not his fault if he doesn't like me anymore.

No, LP! Don't give him excuses! He's just brainwashing you again.

It's not illegal to change your mind—yet.

I mean, think about it, you guys. I mean, really think about it. It could happen. It really could. I mean, think about it.

It's just kind of painful, you know, and I've just spent the past couple of days healing. Writing and sleeping and crying, my basic pattern. I learned something: some really fucking great writing comes from pain.

Fuck. Yeah.

I'm just worried that he thinks I hate him or something—which I sure as hell don't. I remember right before he told me it wasn't going to happen—

Going down memory lane already! See, Homeroom Boy, we've already shared so much! How can you just throw it away like this?

—he asked me what I thought of him, how I felt about him. Had he not already started with some bad news, I probably would have told him. I wouldn't have hesitated. I've only said it three other times before in my life but I know that this one would have even more meaning, more feeling than the others.

My apologies to the other three boys, just in case you're reading this. It's possible at least one of you might read this some day. But not you, Thirty-Six Hours Boy. You can go suck a nut. Try doing that while you're feeling so "tied down."

I would have straight out said it: "I love you." But I didn't. I sat there like a dumb-ass and made us both feel like shit.

[HOMEROOM BOY], I hope he isn't pissed at me or at himself. How do I tell him that he didn't do anything wrong and that no matter what happens I'll always be there for him? How do I tell him I care without him freaking out? How do I tell him that he's my best friend in the whole world and that I need him?

Maybe I already did.

Pam

It gets worse from there. Okay, sorry, I know you need a second from that "Maybe I already did." Go ahead. Put the book down and take a breath and thank time and space for making it so that you are no longer fifteen and that when you *were* fifteen you weren't near me, or if you were near me when you were fifteen, at least find some comfort in the fact that you weren't *actually* me. When you pick this book up again (*Please? Share with me my soul?*) I will start with something that might make you need to take a break again.

Are you back? Okay. So after I finished writing that letter, what I did next was...

I called him.

I mean, I immediately called him.

I finished this FIVE PAGE SINGLE-SPACED LETTER and then picked up my phone and punched in his digits. And then I read it to him over the phone.

You guys.

I READ THIS LETTER TO HIM OVER THE PHONE.

Every word. I read him the entire thing. Without stopping. Without even checking to see if he hung up at any point. I just barfed up my weepy, fainty heart.

There was a pause after I finished the last word. That last word being, "Pam," in case he was unsure who was talking to him. There was a pause. A pretty long one, if I recall. And then he said:

"I have to go."

"Oh, okay, yeah, I understand."

That was the last time Homeroom Boy ever spoke to me. I cannot blame him for that choice. I can't even blame the alphabet. That one was all on me.

How To Smell Like Holly Hunter Boy
(a recipe)

Ingredients:
    1 Bottle of Pert Plus
    1 container of Arrid X-tra Dry (powder fresh scent)
    1 bar of Irish Spring soap
    1 bottle Drakkar Noir (optional, for special occasions, like
    school dances)

Directions: Slap that shit all over your body. Bathe yourself in it. Drown yourself. Apply generously. Sniff yourself constantly. Squirt Drakkar Noir on your own watchband so that you can smell your soul mate every time you daydream about him, mentally floating hundreds of miles away at your school desk, your hand on your chin. Casually find a way to learn the laundry detergent his mother uses or you're never going to get that pillowcase to smell like him, no matter how hard you hug that pillow at night.

    Reapply as needed.

    (It's always needed.)

A couple of weeks pass with no two-hundred page letter in the mail from Holly Hunter Boy and no email explaining its absence. Since apparently I am still that same girl who yearned for heat stroke at Six Flags, I email Holly Hunter Boy, trying to be all *super-caszh*:

Hello!

I had a dream last night that you tried to send the 200 page letter, but it got lost in the mail. This morning, I could no longer remember if it was a dream. Part of that is because I've been writing around this time in our lives, and it's really weird going back into my teenage headspace.

—p

PS I'm really sorry about the time I made you listen to an entire Edie Brickell & the New Bohemians song over the phone.

It is a little *yikes*-inducing that I'm still all, "*Was it a dream?*" with my communication to this man.
He replied:

I haven't located the note yet. I know the box that it's in and don't have it yet. (BTW It's stored at my mother's house. She has used this opportunity to unload everything that I have stored there—except said box.)

I saw something the other day that made me think of you. Something on Facebook said that this generation will never know hanging up angrily. They will just push a button on their iPhone. It made me think of the time that you made me so mad that I threw my phone down and it broke. I think you said that Metallica sucked. Bitch. I hope my son never slams down his hologram iPhone while talking to your daughter.

I'll send note as soon as I locate it. In the meantime feel free to ask any questions. And we should talk soon.

Then I wrote the following:

Haha, I don't remember that story, but that's fantastic. There is no way I meant what I said, unless I was talking about their post Black Album work, in which case I stand behind that statement.

This morning I was trying to figure out what kind of questions to ask you without embarrassing myself all over again. In line with the themes/epiphanies I've been tinkering with, how about:

What is your earliest memory of me? Meaning, how and when did you first notice me?

How would you have defined our relationship in the sixth grade?

At a certain point you had to know I "liked you" liked you. Did it hit you at once, dawn on you, or was it clear because I told you?

What did you think when you started getting all these notes from me?

Did you ever think of trying to let me down gently?

I seem to remember you always having a girlfriend. Was there ever a time you decided to keep a girlfriend around just a little longer than you wanted just to make sure you weren't available, or is it possible I am giving myself way too much real estate in your mind/heart that I never actually possessed?

Do you remember watching Broadcast News with me?

I don't remember if the 200 page note was your idea or mine. Do you? And what did you think when you got it?

Why did you keep it?

And then I hit send and then I said out loud, "WHAT HAVE I DONE?" because basically I just re-opened all my old wounds. What if I don't want to know the answers to these questions? What am I doing? Why don't I ever learn?

How will I know the difference in my writing now and my writing then when I'm basically sitting on the floor writing the same questions about the same boy? But instead of a notebook I'm now using…oh, God, it's still called a notebook even though it's a computer!

Are you now reading this with one eye closed and a hand over your face? You are? Oh, good, so it's not just me with regrets?

Maybe that's progress. Maybe I should just let all my anxieties go and just trust that whatever answers come back in an e-mail, if any at all, they'll be the ones that I need to read, that I need to hear. Maybe I'll can just be confident that instead of starting up a whole new realm of personal mortification, instead of needing three more years of intense therapy to undo some self-esteem issues, I can be proud of myself that I'm brave enough to find out the answers to questions I've wondered for decades. Maybe I can consider myself lucky that I even have someone in my life who's known me this long, who would be kind enough to take time out of his day to once again answer something much longer than it should be, directed too intensely at him. Isn't this what everybody would want, if given the chance? Don't they write movies and novels about this very desire? It's not a "do over," I'm not looking to fix what happened, I just want to know if it was as bad as I remember. Wouldn't we all want to know that, if we could? So maybe I should just stop for a second, calm down, and tell myself everything will be okay.

…Maybe I already did.

Too Many People,
Too Noisy, Too Noisy

It's hard to know right from the beginning if this is a letter, a short story, a diary entry, or a panic attack.

6 Nov., 1990

I don't want to be here anymore. I can't stay here anymore. I don't like it here. It's not good. It's just not good. I can't think.

Maybe I'm talking about being at home?

I can't move. I can't breathe. I'm dying. I'm dying here. I'm dying and I need help.

I'm probably talking about being fifteen. Or I just watched the video for Metallica's "One" again.

I need air. I need space. I need to be alone. Why won't everyone leave me alone? Why are they bothering me? Why are they making me do things I don't want to do? I want to leave. I don't want to be here anymore. Too many people. Too noisy. Too noisy. People screaming, people laughing, people yelling, people moving.

"*Land mine!*" Wait. Maybe I'm talking about school? Am I in homeroom?

Moving around me. Circling me. Chanting. Yes, they
are chanting and teasing and throwing things. Food.

I'm fucking writing about the cafeteria? Seriously? I mean, I
guess I needed to work through some stuff after not getting one of
School Bus Boy's apology letters, but—

Why do they throw food, I don't need food. I need to be
free! I need to be able to leap and run and—

Oh, no. I'm writing about animals at a zoo. Jesus, how is it
always worse than I think it'll be? Always!

—walk and yell and sleep and eat when I want to. Why
won't anyone listen to me? Why won't they listen? Why?
Let me go! Somebody! Anybody! I'm trapped here in
this cage! I'm locked in here, you see?

What if I gave this to somebody? There's a really good chance
I stuffed this into a locker and was all crazy-eyes, going, "DO YOU
LIKE IT/ME?"

You stare and laugh and point and talk about me but
can't you see I'm in misery? Can't you see that? Can't
you? I'm not happy here in this damn faux nature
scene. You think this is a real tree that I nap under?
Hell, no. It's plastic. Even a real tree can't live under
these hellish conditions.

What? Why would the tree be plastic? Am I a fish?

I can't breathe. Maybe if I had a tree or two I could get
some oxygen in here! Stop laughing! Stop pointing! I
am not cute! I am not happy!

Look, no matter what I thought I was writing about, it is clear
that I was really just writing about being fifteen.

Can't you see that isn't a glimmer in my eye? It's a teardrop. I'm crying. I'm unhappy and I'd like to leave. Please. Please. I didn't do anything wrong. I just want to leave. I did nothing wrong. I was taken here because of *what* I am, not *who* I am. I am not one of you and because of that I am stuck here in this simulated environment alone. Alone. I just, I, I don't like it here.

What if I wrote this to be a monologue? What if I performed it and I've just blocked it from my memory?

I'm frightened. I don't like it here. When will you listen to me? When will somebody help me? Do I look like I'm kidding? I am an animal that deserves to be free! I did no wrong. My only vice is fur!

So: not a fish. I was contributing to no less than four different animal rights groups at this time. I tried to be a vegetarian, which lasted about a month when my parents grounded me until I ate meat. My moral code wasn't as strong as my desire to hang out in the parking lot of a strip mall on Friday nights. Don't judge me. If you'd lived at my house, yours wouldn't have been either.

I don't point and stare at you. Please leave me alone. I can make you leave my sight. I can. All I have to do is close my eyes. Watch. See, I told you. I can't see you anymore. But you are still pounding in my ears and vibrating through my brain forcing your chants into my soul.

I think we're going to need to do a "soul" count in these letters.

I can still feel your laughter through my bones and occasionally feel the pounding of cheap "food" pegged at my head. I told you. I don't need food. I need freedom. Please. I don't like it here anymore.

It just ends here, so hopefully that means I got up and went outside.

Stalking the Clueless

Dec. 1990

[HOLLY HUNTER BOY]…

Hello. Right now I'm stuck at my mom's hotel with nothing to do. Well, except write letters, because my mom gave me a lump of stationary [*sic*] & said, "be creative, write a story." Of course, I have writer's block.

The ellipses! Such a mysterious way to begin my sexy correspondence. Here I am, showing this boy that despite my mother's request for me to write stories, I'm instead sneaking away to pencil a few words to my beloved, who lives hundreds of miles away from me and has a girlfriend.

I went to a party Friday night. I met this guy named [----]. He's 18, and right now he's on a plane on his way to college. He's going to be a biophysicist. Wow. Anyway, he was telling [K], [----], and me the way you can tell when a guy is worth talking to. He also showed us really neat ways to hurt people. But enough about him…

This has brought back a memory that I had completely buried in my mind. It's nice that here I'm obviously trying to get my long distance friend to ask me about this older gentleman who taught me a few things on a Friday night (you know, because I used ellipses again), but I also remember that this guy gave me some bullshit line about how if only he wasn't going to college, he'd totally fall in love with me. And also called me a prude when I wouldn't let him go down on me in the dark in a bedroom that had two other girls in it who were trying to sleep (sex lives of the youth!). When I insisted he stopped trying to take off my pants, he whispered, very wetly and quite loudly, deep into my ear hole, "*Why won't you let me eat you?*"

That haunts me to this day. I still remember how gross every second of that felt, so close to my head, my brain, my soul. So close to my friends, who were truly about five feet away, obviously not sleeping, trying to block out their present situation, hopefully with super-thick pillows.

> How are you? See, you didn't write to me, so I shouldn't be sending you this. [---] also didn't write back.

The letter ends there, as if I just talked myself out of continuing further because all of my pen pals have been ignoring my pleas for correspondence.

Don't worry, I found a way to drum up some new inspiration, because immediately a new page begins:

> "Hi. I'm Eric."

> Hi, I'm speechless.

I have no doubt I swiped that from a sitcom. If I didn't, I'm using it in a future one.

> I just stared at the blonde god in front of me. I looked around to see if he was talking to someone else. He wasn't.

> "You do speak English, right?" His blue eyes sunk deep into my brain, and I will never see a more beautiful color for the rest of my life.

> I gave a small giggle. "Karen. My name is Karen." I repeated it to kind of reassure myself that I was Karen.

Hee heeeeeee. I guess I stalled out with Karen's story, or got distracted talking to my mom or something, because I then begin again. There's a distinct theme.

> "Kacie," The blonde god whispered in my ear. "Kacie," he said a little louder. "Kacie!" he started shouting in my ear, his voice slightly changing. "Kacie!" Now it was more of a cackly [sic] voice. "Kacie!" Now I recognized the voice. "Kacie!"
>
> It was my mother's voice.
>
> "Kacie! Hurry up if you want to go to the movies!"
>
> A sort of haze filled my mind as the blonde god left my side to go back to his little nook in the dream state.

I don't know what I'd been reading that got the phrase "blonde god" in my head. There were a few years where I read *Tiger Beat*s, but I never really got into them, as I wasn't interested in pictures of the New Kids on the Block or Jason Priestley. I wanted pictures of Johnny Depp and the Beastie Boys, and for that I had to tear up issues of *Rolling Stone*.

I suppose that only makes me cool in retrospect. At the time it made me so, so weird.

At the end of my freshman year I had made friends with some serious New Kids on the Block fans. I'm talking die-hard fans. They won contests to meet them and such. My friend Amber was so into them she had covered her room in New Kids. *Coated* her room. Every single available space in her room was plastered. The light switch was a picture of Donnie Wahlberg and his crotch was over the switch, so when you would turn on the light, Donnie would be very happy to see you. She had an 18×18 tapestry over her bed. Her closet walls were covered. But she still wasn't satisfied. She needed more pictures, newer pictures, *every picture*.

So Amber had an idea.

"You know, there's these ads you can put in the back of the *Tiger Beat* so that you can trade pictures with anyone around the world," she said. We were sitting around the lunch table, so you can imagine this like a much younger version of a *Sex and the City* cold open. "You tell them what you want, and you give them what they want in return. Since we have so many magazines with all these pictures that we don't want, we could go into a photo trading business."

"I hate the New Kids," I said.

"Yes, but you love Johnny Depp. And I know that most people would trade, like, *five* Johnny Depps for a Chad Allen."

Her point was solid.

"I don't have any of those *Tiger Beats*," I said.

"No, but you have *Rolling Stone*. So you get all the Sting and Beastie Boys and Aerosmiths—"

"Eww," our friend Amy said. "Who likes Aerosmith?"

"Joe Perry is cute," I mumbled very quietly.

And we were in business.

Crazy for the Kids.
Looking for Pictures of
New Kids on the Block and Johnny Depp.
Have extensive collection to trade.
Send requests to...

Amber must have placed the ad in *every* teen magazine in existence, because in about two weeks we started getting letters. Lots of letters.

(For those of you who are fifteen now, I should explain. "Letters" are these articles of communication that would arrive at our homes via something called "the mail." We didn't have the "e" part of mail yet. And yes, we used to want pictures from magazines so much we would spend money to send them to each other. Try to imagine if you had to pay a quarter every time you wanted to post something to Tumblr. It's a little like that. Hmm? What did you say? Oh, yes. Yes, that's fucking stupid. You are correct.)

Our collection was extensive. We were very meticulous. We had a file system of all the pictures arranged alphabetically for every celebrity we could think of. We tore through our magazine collections to create this database of skin. We had over three hundred photos and articles. We were ready.

Or so we thought.

The letters were simple at first.

"*I have six New Kids photos and one Johnny Depp that I can send to you if you send me six Balthazar Gettys. Please reply as soon as possible, and I will send you all I have.*"

Six Balthazar Gettys? That's a pretty tall order. I noticed that this girl had not sent a self-addressed stamped envelope. I went back through our ad...no mention of a SASE.

(Youthful readers: remember that quarter for a Tumblr analogy I gave you earlier? Now imagine someone had to also pay a quarter to repost your Tumblr post. Now imagine you somehow forgot to add the PayPal button and instead you were just being charged that quarter for every repost or heart-button click. (Is it called "love," that click? Do I sound old? I'm not old. I swear, I'm not old. BUT I LOVED JOHNNY DEPP BEFORE YOU WERE A FETUS.))

So. No SASE. I was livid. "Amber, how can you not ask people to send that? Do you know how many stamps we are going to need?"

(Stamps are...just ask your parents.)

Amber wasn't fazed. "I'm sure they know to do it, most of these girls have done this before. Hand me that Mariah Carey."

We had a form letter we would send out to our interested parties with a checklist menu. They'd mark what they wanted, send the NKOTB and/or Depp with their requests, and in a week or so, their order would be filled.

Simple, right? It was.

Until Amber went on vacation. Her parents took her to Maine or something for about a month. That left the business solely in my hands.

"Don't sweat it," she said to my panicked face, right before she abandoned me. "Just send this checklist, then send what they want when it comes back. I've started putting your address on everything coming in, and just check my mail every day for the new ones from the magazines."

Within a week I was sitting in my bedroom looking at sixty-five requests for different celebrities. I was surrounded by handwritten pages of lust and greed. My fingers were covered in paper cuts. I was also looking at two hundred pictures of the New

Kids and like, **six** Johnny Depp photos. SIX! Three of which were the *Sassy* poster that they sent out on a promotional campaign to every girl who ever bought a magazine, so I already had that poster on my ceiling.

Not only was I in over my head, I wasn't getting anything in return. I needed money. More importantly, I needed stamps.

"I am not buying you another book of stamps," my mother said. "You've already spent over thirty dollars in stamps."

She didn't even know the half of it. I had spent fifty of my own money on top of the thirty I'd borrowed from my mother. Before she left, Amber had spent another sixty on top of that for stamps, envelopes, and checklist paper.

While Mom was furious that I was left with all of this work while Amber was racking up New Kids pics while on vacation, I had to admire Amber's business skills. She knew how to train and flee. Whatever Amber's doing these days, I have no doubt she's successful at it, and probably in charge of at least fifty people.

I spent that summer telling girls that we were out of Luke Perry and we never had any Skid Row. If only this could have all been done by phone.

Wait, scratch that. Long distance bills.

(Youngsters, you used to have to pay extra to talk to people on your phone if they lived outside your city. You will never know the feeling of being on the phone on your back in your college dorm hallway with a kitchen timer on your stomach, counting how many minutes you have left before you've run out of cash on your Long Distance pre-paid credit card. (At my alma mater, University of Texas, UTLD was six cents a minute after nine; twelve cents a minute during peak hours. How I still remember that and cannot tell you right now where my purse is? I'll never understand.))

If only Johnny Depp was as popular as the New Kids. (Kids, Johnny Depp was as popular back then as the New Kids are now.) Amber made out like a bandit, and had enough photos at the end of the year for three scrapbooks. I had two Johnny Depp articles, one amazing picture of him sitting cross-legged smoking a cigarette, where you could see the tattoo of his mother's name, one great poster of him in a white T-shirt staring at me with those "I love only you" eyes, and ten copies of the *Sassy* poster.

It was a nice poster though.

I still have the one of him in the white T-shirt...somewhere. (I'll never tell.) (It's in my garage.)

Back to my short story written on lumps from my mother's hotel. When we last left LP's heroine "Kacie," she had been rudely disturbed from her dream about a blonde god.

> "I'll be there soon." I sort of yelled. I don't think I can get up. I feel nailed to my bed. But I have been waiting to see this Keifer Sutherland film. I blinked my eyes open. I stared at the ceiling. I wonder what time it is.

> I turned my head to the left. 11:30. I have never slept so late before in my life. I had to get up. I'm supposed to be going to see this movie with Eric.

> Eric had the greatest pick-up line: "Do you have any spare lust you could share with me?" A little rude, but if you saw him you'd forgive him instantly. Piercing dark eyes—almost black eyes. Long brown hair.

It ends there, as I probably went to find a Diet Coke and wander through the hallways of Sheraton Town & Country in Houston, Texas (RIP).

I'm trying to remember if that "greatest pick-up line" was something I came up with or something I heard on the school bus. I'm pretty sure it's the latter. I don't know who the "blonde god" I'm referencing here could be. I'm sure it's someone I saw at that party, or walking past the senior parking lot, or it's Peter DeLuise. With me at that age, who knows?

God, I hope LP got to see that Keifer Sutherland movie.

Next page:

> Kacie could not believe it. This just wasn't possible. How could this happen? Before she could always eat and eat. She went to sleep with her flat tummy and trim thighs, and she woke up

And SCENE!

I must have been struck with inspiration, as it now changes from the stationery to pages torn from my spiral notebook. This is a very different love letter because it appears to have been written only to flatter and arouse...myself. Look out for some serious teen-girl fantasy fiction.

"Alli Weatherton, if you eat one more thing I'm gonna hurt you!"

That's what I usually hear. This is usually followed by:

"How you can eat so much and stay so thin is beyond me."

And then:

"You make me sick."

It's a lot of fun, actually. I mean, eating whatever I want, whenever I want. I don't brag about it, of course. But sometimes I feel so sorry for my friends who are constantly on one diet after another.

At the moment I am eating hot fudge sundaes with my best friend, Tricia Colbert. She eats as much as I do. And she shows it too. She decided to skip her diet this evening to celebrate my parents being out of town this weekend.

"So," she said, with her mouth full of ice cream. "How many people are coming to this party?"

"Everyone," I said. It was true. At least sixty people. And that's a lot for this town. Trenton, Rhode Island, is so small of a town that it's not on any map. "Want another sundae?" I asked her, as I stood up.

"No!" Tricia held her stomach and rolled back and forth on my beige carpet, getting tiny dust bunnies caught in her long, kinky, brown hair. "How can you eat so much? You are so thin! That Robert would be a complete moron if he doesn't fall for you immediately."

She's talking about Robert Chase, the guy I'm stoking out at my party tomorrow night. I hope she's right. I grabbed a bag of Oreos from the counter and returned to my seat in front of the television.

You guys, remember when everybody was totally saying "stoking out" after I coined it? I wonder if I thought it meant something that existed.

I wrote myself a fantasy story where I was a girl who could eat anything I wanted without getting fat, and that makes me so sad for LP. I'm hoping if this story had continued, one day Alli would wake up suddenly, tragically fat, and her friend would be thin, and her friend would get to date Robert Chase who would totally be stoking out the skinny girl and not fat Alli.

It's all I wanted, really, to be the pretty, popular girl whom people envied, instead of the weird one always raising her hand or reading a book. I didn't hate myself; I just knew that I wasn't the kind of girl who got attention for simply existing. You know, the girl who's so pretty everybody's talking about her. I had to be like, *HI, I AM IN A PLAY AND NOW I'M READING A POEM AND I'M IN YEARBOOK AND WATCH ME WEAR THIS GREENPEACE SHIRT AND COMBAT BOOTS.* At a certain point I think I just went all-out weird.

For a moment can we pause to recognize the genius of LP trying to get away with a fictional town by saying it was so small it couldn't be found on <u>any</u> map?

My mom never takes enough credit for being the one who got me started writing stories. My dad was an aspiring writer, so I think she assumes I was trying to be like him. But it was my mom who always told me to entertain myself by writing things down. Smart mom: you can't talk while you're writing. I mean, now I can, but it has taken years to acquire the skill.

And Then There's
Super Mario Brothers Boy

This is a big one, this relationship. The one who got away. Then I grabbed him, but he got away (or "escaped") when I tried to put him in something with a lock and key. This boy called me his "special" friend. Not his best friend—that was a girl who lived two houses down from me. He would often go and visit her without stopping by to say hello. I would know that because I'd see him leaving her house sometimes when I was hidden in her bushes.

I was his "special" friend not in that way where we would secretly make out, although those days were to come, much later, but at the time we were super special friends in a way that was uniquely catered to shatter my heart.

Almost every day after school, he would come home with me and we would lock ourselves in a room and for hours and hours we did nothing but sit very very close to each other…and play Super Mario Brothers.

Sometimes it was Tetris. But usually it was Super Mario Brothers. I think we eventually beat the game, but I don't remember a minute of it because I spent the entire time with my heart on overdrive as I wondered *IS THIS THE DAY HE KISSES ME BECAUSE HE FINALLY REALIZES THAT I AM THE PRINCESS HE REALLY WANTS TO SAVE??????*

Nowadays I could tell you that he looks like a softer, younger Dave Grohl. Back then I was a complete sucker for his floppy hair and sad eyes. His skin was flawless and creamy, and he often had flushed cheeks. During the winter of my fifteenth year, this boy had me wrestling some serious hormones. Prepare to shield yourself from my intensity.

20, Jan., 1991

> Look at me. Look into my eyes. Let me look into you.
> Let me look beyond that mask you wear into your real
> feelings—your real fears, your real worries, your real
> joys, your real sorrows, your real wounds, your real
> pride, your real goodness, your real honesty, your real
> gentleness, your real peace, your real turmoil.

It's so urgent! *Let me look into you.* Also said by serial killers right before they cut people open. And look, I know Alanis Morrisette cornered the market on songs that are actually just lists, but as you can see here, I was way ahead of her.

> Let me push aside what you want me to see, and
> examine what you've been hiding from yourself. Why
> are you trembling? Is it because I found it? Is this the
> door that unlocks your secrets?

It still sounds like I'm an actual serial killer who is torturing someone with a knife.

> Will you share them with me? Don't be scared. All I need
> is the key. Please. This door is worse than Pandora's box.

Jesus. I mean actual Jesus just said his own name, he's so embarrassed for me.

> Open it. I want to learn about you. I want to feel your
> mind. I want to hold your fears and take them away
> from you. I want to know about your happy memories.
> I want to comfort you during your sad ones. Don't close
> those eyes. Those tears won't wash the pain away. You
> need me.

You need me legally enforced to be at least five hundred feet away from you at all times. My God. Needless to say the letter abruptly ends here as I threw my journal aside, too upset with the fact that no boy would let me feel his mind. LP most likely went to go find herself a bag of Doritos—another kind of Pandora's box.

I wasn't done that day. I somehow found the strength to write again. A warning: this one's pretty rough. If you were ever in your life a fifteen-year-old girl, this might trigger some PTSD flashbacks strong enough to re-sprout your breast buds.

20, Jan., 1991

I think that this is called depression. I'm not sure. Maybe. I thought you were supposed to cry when you are depressed. How come I'm not crying? I've been sitting here for over to 2 hours now feeling completely empty. I've been listening to old sad songs and just singing along.

Don't worry, LP. In about fifteen years you can do the exact same thing and nobody cares because it's called being drunk.

I wrote several unsigned love letters. I carved things into my skin. I contemplated telling my parents to fuck off. I re-arranged all of my cassette tapes. I counted how many times I inhaled in one minute.

I feel the need to reassure all of you that I'm probably exaggerating, if not flat-out lying. If I carved "things" into my skin, I probably scratched at my ankle with a safety pin, because for some reason back then I thought it would be super cool to have a scab on my leg in the shape of the Red Hot Chili Peppers symbol.

It took more than a week to safety-pin-scratch that symbol on my ankle, and it really hurt. During the day at school, the scab would rip and the raw skin would fuse to my sock. I was torn between taking care of the wound so that I didn't get an infection and letting it just fester and scar so that people could see my pain, this pain disguised as an asterisk encircled by the words "Red Hot Chili Peppers."

I'm quite grateful the scar didn't last, just as much as I'm grateful that at a certain point it's difficult to scratch a lowercase "p" into your ankle, because even though back then I was mostly in Keds or combat boots, these days I really enjoy wearing cute shoes. People will write off the occasional tattoo of regret, but a relic from the organic anti-beatbox band might not impress anybody, including Anthony Kiedis.

I wasn't good at carving, but I was excellent at burning. That was my self-torture of choice, if we're getting real here for a second. [Actual, for real trigger warning] I would flick a lighter and wait until the metal was super hot, and then I'd quickly extinguish the flame and press the metal to the inside of my left wrist. I would do this until the skin would blister, rip, and seep. I would do this until I was crying. I would do this until I couldn't do it anymore. I learned it from Super Mario Brothers Boy (SMB Boy, for short), who had used his own lighter to burn a happy face into the back of his hand. Everybody focuses on girls who cut and maim themselves, but all the cutters and burners I knew in high school were boys. Stressed-out, confused, unhappy boys.

I burned myself when I felt like nobody understood, when I didn't know how to express all the weird feelings inside. I often wonder if everything would have been different if I could've had a blog. An online forum. Facebook. Something to reach the world from my tiny bedroom. If I had called out back then, would someone have listened? Would someone finally give me a reply?

But I didn't have the Internet, carving was painful, and burning left too much of a wound. So I had to stop. Once I'd called whatever boy of the month was receiving my unearned, unrequested affection I'd probably re-arrange all my cassette tapes before finally plopping down on the carpet in front of my daybed to write some more.

> I called you sixteen times and hung up. Well, I almost called you sixteen times. I could always dial the first six numbers, and then I got this uncontrollable feeling of fear, and my trembling hand would slam down the phone before the other one could finish calling you.

I would like to think that this is a lie, but the specificity of the number sixteen makes me worry that I did this, allowing myself only sixteen attempts to call. Oh, and kids: phone numbers used to only be seven numbers long. I know! It's because we didn't each have a phone back then. We shared one for, like, an entire house. Yes, it was ridiculous. Eventually they invented a thing called a "party line." It did not create parties. Ask a grown-up to do an impression of a "busy signal" for you. When I was your age, it was the worst sound in the world.

I carved your name in my bookcase.

You'd think I'd remember doing that, as a bookcase holds my favorite ice cream flavor, but I don't. I do remember, back in Mississippi, a junior high friend of mine carved the name of the boy she liked into my footboard, and I'm still pretty pissed off about it. My bed is not your oak tree, missy. If memory serves, that's the boy I eventually had my first tongue kiss with, which was awkward since his initials were carved into my bed by another girl who had long since decided she no longer found him to be "so fine it hurts." Is it harder to be a teenager in the South? I feel like maybe it is.

I tried meditation. "Maybe this is boredom," I thought, as I curled my legs out of the Lotus position. Then, as I stood up to try and put some excitement back into my life, I saw your picture sitting on my bureau, and I realized that this really was depression.

I didn't have a "bureau." I must confess I'm not enough of a grown-up now to know exactly what a "bureau" is. Is it the same as a dresser? Or does a bureau have doors? Is that an armoire? This letter is confusing me. Not because I have no idea what picture I could be talking about (there's absolutely no way I'd keep a framed photo of a boy on any article of furniture in a building where my dad was within mocking distance), but mostly because I know I didn't try meditation. I couldn't get my legs into the Lotus position; my family had KFC at least twice a week.

The fact that these damn tears keep rolling down my face was pretty much the giveaway.

LP forgot her opening statement.

That and this ripping, gnawing sensation that is tearing at my insides.

…which is probably the KFC.

Maybe that's where my soul is.

Oh, GOD. Why is life so stupid at fifteen? Why did ANYBODY talk to me? Honestly.

Maybe that's where my heart is. No, you know where my heart is, don't you? It's that crumpled piece of paper you tossed aside carelessly onto your desk. It's written on the lines of that sheet of paper. It's the ink that was used to write those three words that didn't even phase [sic] you: I love you. Maybe

And, you know, it just ends there because I'd run out of cheese.

Love Means Never Having to Say Anything: Silent Skateboarder Boy

So here is where I fall in love with someone else. What did it? Well, I suppose it was the way this boy completely ignored me in a very new way. He *never* spoke to me. Not once. Never. I would sit near him on the bus every day and he never spoke. Granted, he was shy and hardly talked to anyone, but he must have felt so awkward sitting so close to me for half an hour Monday through Friday while I stared at him with wide-eyes and crimson cheeks and never once said anything to him. Using my mouth, I mean. My heart was screaming at him. No doubt he could see it trying to climb out of my chest through my throat.

He wore a skate key around his neck. I remember that. He had dark hair, dark skin, and usually wore a white T-shirt. He often carried his skateboard protectively in front of his chest, and he kept his head down. In fact, I have exactly one photograph of him, and it is of his skateboard and his hands. That's because he's using his skateboard to shield his face from my camera—a physical representation of our emotional bond, forever frozen.

I remember his name. I do not need to say it to you, mostly because he never said it to me. But he inspired this:

21, Jan., 1991

Oh, to actually feel your body pressing against mine—
what a heaven that must be. To intertwine my fingers
with yours would only make me more alive than I've
ever been. To gaze for hours deep into your eyes and

to be lost, swimming in your soul could only send me swirling in a fantastic ecstacy [*sic*].

I like that up to here I haven't pressured him to say anything. He could still be sitting on the bus, holding his skateboard, and I could do the rest of the work.

To hear your voice dancing in my ears spins my heart into a frenzy, sending a tingling rush to every nerve and an embarrasing [*sic*] blush to my face. Being near you drives me wild. Talking to you makes me happy. But to actually touch you and to have you touch me…that is the burning desire I have deep in my soul and my sole reason for survival. I need you. I want you.

His first name. His bus route. His best friend. Where he ate lunch. There. I just told you everything I knew about Silent Skateboarder Boy.

Okay, and he had thick, dark hair that looked like it would be really fun to touch. With my *soul*.

When you are away I feel an emptiness—all remnants of happiness are gone and my feeling of euphoria exits at such an alarmingly rapid speed that I feel I'm crashing from some sort of drug that had taken me soaring above the sky, above the world, past all dangers, past all worries, past all sorrows, past all darkness into a whirling, twisting glow and had danced with me and spun me around and around and then dropped me back into my hellish reality. Without you.

One time he got tricked into hanging out with K and me at the parking lot of a Krogers on a Friday night. Maybe not a trick, more of a forced gathering. He and his friend were skating, and K and I just didn't leave them alone. When they looked like they might go find something to do that was anywhere but where we were, we entice-bribed them with tacos.

The four of us sat at a Taco Bell eating tacos while going through the contents of K's purse. Technically, this was my very first date. I still have pictures from that night. There's the one where SSB is shielding himself from me with his board, one of my shoes as I'm running after him, and one of the insides of an overturned purse in a booth at a Taco Bell. It was magical.

But like all things magical, it was over too soon. He got someone to tell someone to tell my friend to tell me that he wasn't interested in me "like that."

And then, quite suddenly, he stopped riding the bus.

THE SEA OF PAIN

27, Jan. 1991

She stood—poised—hands in their familiar position. This time she was determined to do it. This time she'd push all of her fears aside. This time she'd show them all by ending it all. But most of all she'd forget about him.

She'd forget how amazingly wonderful he was. She'd forget how numbing it was to stare into his eyes. She'd forget what his touch was like, what his kisses were like, what his warm breath playing on her cheek was like, what love was like—all would be gone in one swift motion. If only she would just do it.

I'm not sure where I got it into my head that I would enjoy the feeling of someone breathing on my face. It's not great when anybody does it. The love of your life, your dog, your baby—breath is hot and steamy, and smells like whatever was in that mouthhole last. Breath does not "dance." It engulfs. It smothers. It is a boner-killer more powerful than Little Pam with a pen.

This next section is weird and I'm sorry about all the imagery.

She would torture herself—trying to hurt herself into doing it. She had bitten her tongue so many times that it had swollen so much that she could barely talk. She pulled strand after agonizing strand of hair from her head—pulling sections hard enough to draw blood. She dug her fingernails deep into her palm. And she stands here now—once again going back on her promise to herself. She promised herself that the pain would end.

I mean, that is a crazy-looking image, this swollen-tongued, mostly bald girl bleeding from the palms as she stands there thinking about hot breath on her face, "hands poised in their familiar position." I know I thought that was some poetry right there.

But she wasn't ready yet. Anger took over, and she began the torture. Clutching the blade in her quivering left hand, she made a small gash in her right hand index finger. She squeezed it tightly, and watched the swell of redness form, and swirl down her fingertip, tracing a path down to her wrist, and slowly rolling off and forming a sea of pain on the tile of her bathroom floor. She looked at her wrist—the blood had traced the pattern for her.

I was once in Guatemala with a group of Koreans who swore this was the way to cure a stomachache. Bloodletting. I was in the back of a van in the middle of nowhere, watching them prick and bleed their fellow traveler from his fingertips in order to "loosen the bad food from inside his arm." If only I could have bled Silent Skateboarder Boy out of my fingers like I was draining some bad *pulique*.

One small slit. One rapid movement and she'd be lifted from this nightmare and thrown into another world. One simple movement was the most important decision she would ever make. Because she chose the right one. She sliced horizontally, vertically, horizontally again— she wanted no chances of surviving this one—

Teenage girls always want to tell you the "right way" to slit your wrists. It's important to be some kind of expert on where to cut, how to slice, and then what pills you should take, if that doesn't work. They like to constantly feel just a bubble bath away from the end of their lives.

> —and felt a rush flowing from her body, from her heart, and from her soul. She closed her eyes and inhaled deep, the smile creeping larger and larger across her face. She was at peace. She lost her grip on the blade, and it fell, spinning and twirling, into the sea of pain where it bobbed and finally sank as she fell to the floor and was lifted beyond.

I know my crush on The Silent Skateboarder Boy was short-lived, but at the time I thought my pining had been never-ending and forever-lasting (I mean, I fake killed myself for him!), but I quickly went back to pining for Super Mario Brothers Boy, possibly because he actually spoke to me. But right before I did, I tried like crazy to not need him in my life. I spent a good year making bad decisions in an effort to find someone else.

There aren't too many notes to boys from this time because I started going outside. I started doing things at night, which meant meeting boys who didn't just sit next to me in class or ride my bus. My friend K had an actual social life and was kind enough to let me be a part of it.

And that changed everything.

My Year of Dicks

The first time I ever really made out with a boy, like super made out—we were in a bed and no parents were home—I was fifteen and very nervous. He must've sensed that, because he got up to make me more comfortable. He put a record on his player. It was 2 Live Crew's "Me So Horny."

So I asked, "Do you have anything else?"

And he said, "I do. It's something that reminds me of you."

And then he played Richard Pryor's *Live in Concert*, which I now choose to take as a compliment.

So we're making out and then he'd start laughing, and I'd think it was because of me, but it was really something Richard Pryor had just said about eating pussy, but I didn't hear it anyway, because I was too busy thinking really important thoughts in all caps like: *I AM FINALLY MAKING OUT WITH A BOY AND GET READY BECAUSE MY ENTIRE LIFE IS ABOUT TO CHANGE.*

My three-way with Richard Pryor was the first time I'd ever been *all-the-way* felt up, the first time I'd been dry humped, had a tongue jammed in my ear, or any of those things you know will happen to you one day but you don't imagine they'll all happen at once, all right in a row all so fast and sticky and wet and with so many people laughing in the background while Richard Pryor is going on about how white women are polite during oral sex and then suddenly this guy was pulling up my shirt and I just knew this was all going too fast and I kind of collapsed on his chest, shuddering and spasming with an asthma attack until I managed to gasp: *"I'm really terrified."*

The next day that boy *dry-humped-and-told* most of the school, or at least the important people in it. That included his—unbeknownst to me—girlfriend at the time. All I heard about it was that his retelling included the lines: "No, I didn't fuck her. That girl was crying before I ever got her shirt off."

That embarrassing moment forced me to make a real change in my life, one that came with a very grown-up, adult, mature decision.

I decided to lose my virginity.

And thus began what I can only describe as *My Year of Dicks*.

The first dick I ever saw in person, I'm almost positive there was something wrong with it.

It wasn't my first encounter with a penis, it was just the first one I saw in the daylight, with my eyes, in real life and not on television or my dad stepping out of a shower. The first penis in the wild that happened to me—and you will understand why I'm insisting it *happened to me* in a second—was a little bit earlier when I went to see *House Party 2*. K was on-again/off-again with this guy who worked at the theater. After he let K and me into the movie for free, he pulled me aside to take me into another screening room that was showing *The Cook, The Thief, His Wife, and Her Lover*. I guess he wanted to watch me watch naked people? I think it was a novelty at the time, a movie with an NC-17 rating playing next to *Ernest Goes to Jail*. Honestly, I can't even pretend to understand what this guy's game was, because I was so unaware of game at the time.

Case in point: we're standing in the aisle watching movie sex when this guy starts putting his tongue in my ear. No warning, no lead up. My ear was suddenly wet with a near-stranger's mouth. This is really surprising when you're holding a tub of popcorn and wearing a giant white T-shirt that says WORLD PEACE.

So I say something cool like, "Should we be standing here in the middle of all these people while you're doing that to me?" He pulls me aside into a seat and the next thing I know he has put my hand on...you guys, look. It's been many years since I was legally allowed to look at teenage dicks, and I'm not trying to. I'm okay with those years being in my past. I'm just saying all I have is hindsight and lingering trauma because this first one felt enormous and like it was made entirely of plastic. I pulled my hand away, positive that he'd wrapped my fingers around some kind of 20 oz. Diet Coke.

But he's looking at me in the dark of the theatre and says something romantic, like, "You wanted to see *House Party 2* for free, didn't you?"

And I'm like, "Yeah, I guess."

But the truth is I have no idea what to do with this thing he's put in my hand that does not feel like a human part and I also don't understand why he's got me in this movie theater instead of K, so I kind of just sit there watching the movie. He stands up and says, "Come on."

Oh, good, I think. *He's walking me back into my Kid 'N Play movie.*

But instead he pushes me into a supply closet, shuts the door, and kisses me while pushing me onto the floor in the dark and he's trying to pull down my pants and I realize it's going to happen right here. *This is it. In the dark, near a mop,* I think. *On some really cold cement. Wearing my WORLD PEACE T-shirt, I'm going to make this important transition into womanhood with a guy who kind of looks like Keifer Sutherland but that's sort of all I know about him. No time to learn middle names; this moment is too important. Everything will be different now. It's really too big of a moment to keep to myself. I should let this boy know that he's about to change everything for me. This is monumental.*

So I stop him as he's trying to unleash his Coke bottle and I say, "Hey. I just want you to know. This will be my first time."

It was dark, so I couldn't see him, but I heard him sort of stop breathing for a second, I guess to figure how best to respond to this important, wonderful, intimate thing we're about to share.

And then he got up and walked out of the supply closet and never said another word to me ever again.

He did sit between K and me as we watched *House Party 2*. Actually, as I watched *House Party 2* because he eventually took K to the supply closet, where they were gone for quite some time. And I thought to myself, *There's a lesson in here, but I am definitely too stupid to know what it is yet. I'll see if I can work it out through a series of poems about a spurned lover.*

So back to this other penis, the first one I could see in the daylight. Um, I…I don't know. He was young, but not too young, my age, but younger than the Coke Bottle dude, and physically smaller, in like, as a human, but also smaller in like, what I was suddenly looking at and dealing with.

I tried to Google what I could have possibly seen, but Googling "When is a dick not done yet?" or "Penis Development Issues Cocktail Weiner" is not going to give you the search results you're looking for. Trust me.

Okay, so the dick. It was…like a dog treat? Like a snausage? Like when a dog gets excited to see you. But like one of those little dogs, where you feel kind of gross about seeing it while at the same time it seems determined to make you see it? It was like that. Like a pink, angry button that was waving around trying to give me orders but I didn't know what I could touch without making something on him hurt.

He was determined to make this thing happen and I was determined to make this happen because I was going to get this virginity over with and he was cute and you know, non-threatening and he's just trying to jam this thing and I'm lying on the floor of his parents' office on some kind of itchy afghan and I'm thinking, *I feel like I'm playing Operation, but I'm the board.*

Anyway, it didn't happen. And to this day, I don't know if I just found a guy who wasn't done growing his stuff yet or if he had some kind of issue with his parts. I really don't have any dick experience with someone younger than fifteen and I'm really not going to find that kind of stuff out through Google because I am terrified of my search history being used against me in a court of law someday. I mean, unrelated to the kid dicks, but that shit's not gonna help.

There were a couple of near-dick experiences after that, but I'm just going to skip to this part:

I went to a party not long after that. One of those parties where I've told at least six lies to my parents to be there, and the mom who's "watching" over this party is in the corner doing cocaine with some teen boys and her daughter is in her bedroom having sex with her boyfriend. Believe me, this is not the kind of party I would normally go to. I'd never seen cocaine before and I even averted my eyes when I realized what was happening because this is the kind of party that is on a very special episode of something and I'm terrified the cops are going to bust in at any moment (somehow with my disappointed mom and dad because that's what happens on those very special episodes) and I didn't want to have seen anything incriminating. In fact, when K's parents found out she was at this party they made her come home immediately. In order to keep me from getting busted by my own parents, we had to part ways. I stayed at a party filled with strangers while my lifeline went home to begin a lengthy punishment.

I didn't drink or do drugs or even smoke cigarettes, so I'm at this party, sitting on a couch, watching *Mothra vs. Godzilla* because I have no way home. There's a guy sitting on the couch next to me, and he's pretty nice. A punk in a worn-out T-shirt for a band I don't know. He's got a bleached Mohawk and oily skin. Skinny pants, combat boots. He made sure I always had a soda. He asked me if I needed a blanket. He told me he thought my blue eyes were pretty and he loved my pale, white skin. I decided I was going to have sex with him. I wasn't going to do drugs or get wasted and there was an eighty-five percent chance I was going to be grounded in the morning for being there, so I figured: *I will make out with this nice boy until he transforms me into a woman.*

We started kissing only after everybody had disappeared or gone to sleep (although there may have been other people sleeping in the room), and I remember finding it odd that he didn't want to take off his combat boots, even though we were sharing a sleeping bag. If he was about to be on top of me, I wasn't sure I wanted combat boots all up in that situation. But he was adamant, said they were too much of a pain in the ass to take off, and I figured maybe he was nervous about foot odor.

He went back to complimenting my eyes, the color of my skin, my blonde hair. "You're perfect," he said. We're kissing, we're hugging, it's kind of sweet and I literally have no idea where I am as I start thinking about how exciting it was that I was making such a grown-up decision. It made me feel so *womanly*, how I was going to just have sex with this mohawked stranger in boots, and I wanted him to know just how amazing this moment was, how very French film we were, so I got really close to his ear and said,

"I can't believe I'm doing this with you. I mean, here we are. Here you are. About to take my virginity. *You will be my first time.*"

He stopped, rolled over onto his back, and—with a very long sigh—he said, "Good night."

We got a ride home the next morning from the girl hosting the party. After she dropped him off at his house, she turned to me and asked, "Did you two do it last night?"

"No," I said. "I guess he's too much of a gentleman. He seemed to want to wait until the time was right, maybe more special."

"Because you know he's a Skinhead, right?"

His combat boots had white laces and he was really into my skin, specifically the color of it, and I shuddered with the realization that I'd almost lost my virginity to a white power supremacist.

My year of dicks was starting to piss me off.

The Skinhead was a sign that I needed to step back and reassess. (Now there's a sentence that I can't believe I just wrote about my past.)

So I went legit. I got a boyfriend. A boyfriend my mother absolutely hated. Like, deep passion hated. She hated him for nothing other than the way he looked, which made me love him so much more. Is there anything that can fuel teenage love more than a mother's disdain? I think not.

Anyway, I knew there was a possibility that we might eventually have sex together, because we'd been totally dating for at least three weeks.

One day I was sitting in the garage with my mother going through boxes, getting ready for a yard sale, when I thought about how I was getting older and we were going to run out of these moments, these mother-daughter moments where we could really talk. She could give advice and I could listen and we would just totally, totally get each other.

So I say, "Hey, Mom? How old were you when you lost your virginity?"

And she looks at me. She looks me right in the eyes and she says, "You shut up. You shut the fuck up right now."

She left the room for about five minutes.

When she returned, she was awkwardly composed as she announced, "Your father would like to speak to you in the living room."

In the living room, my father's sitting on his recliner with a tumbler of Old Grand-Dad in hand. He's smoking a cigarette and looking a little pale.

I take a seat on my skateboard on the floor in the middle of the room and this is where one of the most traumatic experiences of my entire life begins.

LITTLE PAM
You wanted to see me?

DAD
Your mother tells me you are thinking about having sex.

LITTLE PAM
No, Dad, I was just trying to have a—

He does this hand gesture, which means all of what he's about to say is way more important than anything I was about to.

DAD
Regardless. Let's just say that you are thinking about having sex.

LITTLE PAM
Right. But, Dad, I'm not.

DAD
But we'll say you are.

LITTLE PAM
Why? Why do we have to do that?

DAD
Pamela, what makes you think that you are ready to have sex?

LITTLE PAM
Well, if I was ready—

DAD
Umm-hmmm.

LITTLE PAM
It would be because I am in love and I'm ready to move the relationship to the next level.

DAD
Okay. But what makes you think that you would like sex?

Valid question, I guess.

LITTLE PAM
Well, uh, lots of people have sex, and um…they seem to like it…on television. I mean, I haven't seen anybody having sex, it's not like people are inviting me to watch, heh-heh, so this information is all, you know, from books and movies and not like, porn, I don't watch porn, other than like, like soft stuff like Cinemax or—have you read *Endless Love?*

DAD
Pamela, let me ask you a question. Have you ever experienced an orgasm?

Okay, if you have never been directly asked by a parent if you've had an orgasm, I'm going to tell you what it's like.

Your brain starts making a lot of loud sounds to try to drown out what's happening while your body triggers a reflex, somewhere right around your stomach, it's like a diaphragm kind of thing, where you're sort of just only able to make sounds like, *"NO, NO, NO, NO, NO, NO, NO, NO, NO."*

Which is I guess what I was saying when Dad waved his hand.

DAD
So you're saying you've never masturbated or anything?

NOOOOOOOOOOOOO, DAD! I HAVE NOOOOOOT! WHYYYYY IS THIS HAPPENIIIIING TOOOO MEEEEEEEEE?

I mean, what kind of bonding moment was he looking for here?

"Yeah, dad. I've masturbated. Love it. It's the best."

"Oh, good. I know. Do you just use the hand or…?"

"Yeah, mostly. But I like shower massagers, too. I mean, that's always good."

"Oh, yeah. We've got a great one in our master bath, if you'd ever like to try it."

"Thanks, Dad."

"You're welcome, Pam."

"Oh, almost fucked a Skinhead the other night."

"Happens to the best of us, sweetheart."

Anyway, so Detective Dad has concluded that I have no concept of what sex will feel like, due to the lack of my orgasm and touching-myself skills.

DAD
Do you know how I lost my virginity?

So now I'm having the talk I thought I was going to have with my mother with my father instead. Maybe I could work with this. There's something here that could still be healthy, right? Graphic, definitely, and maybe a bit uncomfortable but, you know, how progressive! A father and daughter having The Big Chat. Kinda sweet, when you think about it.

DAD
My buddies took me to a prostitute and told me I couldn't leave until I had sex with her.

Or not. Or it would be one of the top ten worst days of my life.

DAD
I don't even remember her name. She had a lot of back acne and really dark nipples that I didn't find attractive. You had a teacher once who looked a lot like her. I think her name was Karen. The hooker, not your teacher.

LITTLE PAM
Please stop talking.

DAD
Pam, let me tell you something. Women don't actually *like* having sex. What the woman likes is the foreplay before the sex, touching her, teasing her, rubbing on nipples, clitoral stimulation, very sensual, deliberate moves designed for her pleasure. So she likes the hugging and cuddling afterward in the glow following sex. But the penetration of sex on a woman is just…it's quite painful. It's very aggressive and it can be shocking and invasive and there's often chafing and tearing and then lots of blood, especially when your vagina is so young and inexperienced, like yours.

Oh, if you're wondering what I'm doing while he's saying all of this, I mostly just look like I'm trying to stare at the other side of the world. And there's this screaming in my head. It wails: *"WHYYYY IS THIS HAPPENING TO MEEEEEE?"*

DAD
I'll tell you something, Pam, the male penis doesn't know the difference, really, between a vagina, a hand with a little Vaseline in it, or a rubber doll.

Look, I have a lot of regrets about that day, but one of them has to be that right then I didn't ask Dad about the cocktail wiener dick, because he was clearly in the mood to tell me some things, and other than you fine people I've never talked about it before and it haunts me more than Dad's hooker story.

So Dad's telling me that men could just fuck any old thing, like literally an empty toilet paper roll or a hollowed out watermelon or just like, a fresh pan of Jiffy Pop, I don't know. And he's going on about how that's so very different from the complicated machinery inside a woman.

Then he shifts a bit in his chair, leans forward. Dad's getting real, y'all. And he puts his elbows on his knees as he lifts his hands in this gesture I wish I could forget and he says:

DAD
Now your *mother*...xxxxxxxxxxxxx easily.

Please allow me to explain this censorship.

I've told this story too many times for my mother to be comfortable, and I used to perform it live, and I've never censored this statement before. I have to say it's only as I've gotten older that I've realized just how weird and gross it is that my father launched into a description of my mother's sexual excitement for him, so I'm just going to blur out a little bit of that sentence, just to make it less vulgar.

Maybe I just made it even more vulgar, I'm not sure. But I just can't take seeing those words in print, the ones that talk about my mother between the sheets.

Believe me, the omitted words live on in my head. Oh, trust me. They're there. So very *there*. Forever. Scarred synapses, charred in the shape of my mother's parted thighs.

Anyway, I know he said things after that but I don't remember them. I was very far away thinking about how I'd made some poor choices that led to this moment and I just wanted to know if there was any way to think yourself to death, if you could make your brain just stop your heart right there on your skateboard in the living room as your father lights another cigarette and keeps on telling you about how your mother doesn't really like sex, and you have this weird moment where you wonder if your dad also has the unfinished growing dick and is that why your mother is so sexually unsatisfied and maybe that's why she overreacted when you accidentally broke that vase in the kitchen because she's not getting fucked but now you know so much about your parents that emancipation seems like the only way to get through the rest of your life and—*WHYYYY IS THIS HAPPENING TOOOO MEEEEEEEE??*

DAD

So, I think that you and That Boy should just have *oral sex* for a while. Just try that out. If you feel that you need more after say, a month, come back and talk to me some more, and we'll see if you are ready to move on.

Dad's just my sex pharmacist now, giving me a prescription. My spiritual guide on the way to vaginal penetration. And I love how he's suggesting everything to keep that dick away from my God Hole. "*So, you guys liked oral? You think you'd be okay with anal? Okay, here's a pamphlet and some lube. Could be a little rough at the beginning, so give it a couple of weeks and then let me know how it goes and we'll see where we take it from there.*"

Dad ended this speech with a pleased: "Good talk."

I found a way to stumble down the hall, passing my mother without making any eye contact. Then I locked myself in my bedroom and didn't come out until I was a freshman in college.

The good news is that my dad's sex talk officially ended my year of dicks, because I mean, fuck it. It's just not worth it. I was fine with being a virgin forever. I didn't want to know any more about Coke bottle dicks or mini-dicks or my dad's dick. I was done. I went back to saving myself for true love, which meant I was destined to encounter a whole lot of dick moves.

Me, My Boy Drums, and You.

I have to assume the following letter is unsent. I *want* to assume it's unsent. I have a lot of hope that it's unsent. I'm going to at least pretend it's unsent and ask you to do the same. Because the truth is it's a print-out from a dot-matrix printer, which means I wrote it on my Atari ST, which means I probably printed it twice, giving one to the intended recipient. Honestly, the only thing that kept me from several embarrassing situations with that computer is that I was the only person in the house who knew how to use it.

Paranoid (*and intuitive!*) that technology would change, thinking perhaps a floppy disk wasn't the best place to preserve one's heart, I kept a physical copy of this letter for myself. P.S. I have EVERY computer and laptop I've ever had stored in my garage. Do you need a clamshell Mac? Well, you can't have it because I need all those *South Park* .WAV files for the rest of my life.

Behold what might be the most embarrassing thing I've ever found from my past.

5. Feb., 1991

[SUPER MARIO BROTHERS BOY]—

I'm practicing my typing. Told my dad that it is for homework.

Just a cool, casual, breezy chick, ditching some homework, like all the cool girls do.

I know that [SOME BOY] will be calling soon. [K] tells me that I should give him a chance, that if I don't like him after we go out on Friday, then I can just forget him.

Here's all that I remember about this "Some Boy" I'm talking about:
1. His favorite band was Rush. He would talk about it *all the time*. All the time. To this day I've never listened to a Rush song, all because of this guy.
Oh, and the reason I'm mentioning the phone here is because the entire time we were sort of not really dating, we'd only sort of met in real life once.
2. He told me he "loved [his] guitar so much that if it had a hole [he] would fuck it." I'm sure that line worked on somebody. It did not work on me.
3. This date I'm talking about here was at the Taco Bell. That Taco Bell got a lot of teenage action.

Seeing as how I have to double if I am to go out with him—

My parents didn't let me date at fifteen. In order to go somewhere with a boy, I had to make it sound like it was just a bunch of friends all going out for tacos. Which it was.

—then [K] will be there, and she told me that she can always tell when I'm not crazy over a guy (like [SCHOOL BUS BOY] and [ANOTHER GUY I SORT OF DATED BUT WASN'T REALLY SURE IF WE WERE DATING AND LATER HE CLAIMED WE MOST CERTAINLY NEVER DID DATE AT ALL AND ONE DAY YEARS LATER AT A DENNY'S HE PRETENDED HE DIDN'T KNOW WHO I WAS. I HATE HIM AND HE HAD A STUPID NAME THAT RHYMED.]) and she said I won't get into anything I can't handle. But from what I've heard, he's a real girl freak, and a real sex maniac kind of guy and I know that if I do end up going out with him, I may end up losing my virginity to him, which is exactly what I don't want to do.

By the way, this Taco Bell date never happened. I think after I wrote this letter I might have immediately called this sex maniac girl freak and canceled, so that I didn't accidentally lose my virginity in a Taco Bell parking lot in a car with all my friends watching. I mean, that's what happens on television, you guys. How was I supposed to assume it would be any different for me? Then I'd get pregnant because it was my first time and I'd lose that scholarship to Harvard and I'd end up working at that Taco Bell.

...Actually, I did end up working at that Taco Bell. (I'm telling you, this was a small town). I worked there for exactly two days. And then someone sprayed me with the kitchen hose to "initiate" me and I saw how everybody who worked there had massive scars up and down their forearms from repeatedly scalding themselves on the giant vats they use to boil *everything on the menu* out of its stored, dehydrated state.

Also they said overtime was mandatory, so fuck that shit.

> You know how important this whole deal is to me and what scares the hell out of me is that I almost went ahead and did it with [SNAUSAGE DICK] (except that he was "inconsiderate").

"This whole deal" = sex. Losing my virginity. I'm trying to make it sound casual where I admit in the exact same sentence that I'm terrified about it. I lied about Snausage Dick and said I didn't have sex with him because he wouldn't wear a condom. I lied to protect his weird weiner, because I really am a nice girl who never got one thank you from all those dicks that didn't make it inside me.

> I know now that it would have all been for shit, and I probably would have ended up getting hurt. I don't know, I promised [HOLLY HUNTER BOY] I'd save myself for him, but the way things look, I may be destined to be a virgin for life.

I think you know where this is going.

I have to pause here to wonder if Holly Hunter Boy even knew I was saving myself for him. Did I ever tell him? No doubt I found some awkward way to do exactly that.

> I really don't think I'll ever see him again, and even if I do, I know he'll be a different person, one that I may no longer love. I mean, I'll love him, I'll always love [HOLLY HUNTER BOY]—when I do fall in love with someone it usually is forever, actually it is forever—

Man, where did I pick up this line? And did I really think it would work? On *BOYS*?

> —which is why I usually put up with so much shit from guys that I love: I did it with [SILENT SKATEBOARDER BOY] and I did it with [THAT 2 LIVE CREW ASSHOLE WHO TOLD ALL MY FRIENDS I AM A PRUDE].

> People get pissed at me, "Why do you let him do that to you?" "How can you even speak to him, much less care about him?"

Those of you who know me in real life might be going, "Are you fucking kidding me? I just said that to her like, LAST YEAR." [*This message brought to you by Change.* Change: People can't.]

> And saying, "Because I love him," really doesn't count for much in other's eyes. But I moved away from [HOLLY HUNTER BOY], and [THIRTY-SIX HOURS BOY] moved away from me.

You have to kind of admire how poetic I could be in my revisionist history.

> And I am really glad, because I know that if I still lived in [WHERE I WENT TO JUNIOR HIGH], I'd never look at another guy even if [HOLLY HUNTER BOY] was screwing every girl in the state (Even though it's

probably not possible, seeing as how he is still a virgin as well).

How do I even know that? But more importantly: what am I *doing* here? I'm painting this romantic abusive relationship while still trying to protect what I imagine is the reputation of this other guy I "promised" myself to, so that this guy I'm clearly trying to lose my virginity to would know that my forever-love is reserved for guys who understand how precious and important virginity loss is.

THIS is why I don't have any memory of Chemistry class. Because my head was filled with this. What a waste. I could have been learning Spanish. Something I actually need and would help every single day. *Dios mio. (Mia? No learn Spanish me.)*

> And if [2 LIVE CREW BOY] stayed here I'd probably forgive the son of a bitch and still be crying every night wondering when he's going to love me again. I know that all [2 LIVE CREW BOY] wanted me for was sex, I'm not stupid and I'm not blind. But sometimes my heart and my head don't agree, actually most of the time my heart and my head don't agree. OKAY, SO THEY NEVER AGREE. I LIVE BY FOLLOWING MY HEART WHICH ALWAYS GETS ME IN TROUBLE BECAUSE IT IS ALWAYS WRONG AND ALWAYS HURTS ME BUT I CAN'T HELP IT BECAUSE I'M A HOPELESS ROMANTIC AND I'VE ALWAYS WANTED SOMEONE TO ACTUALLY BE IN LOVE WITH ME BECAUSE I THINK IT WOULD BE A KIND OF INTERESTING EXPERIENCE BUT I WOULDN'T KNOW BECAUSE NO ONE LOVES ME FOR LONGER THAN TWO WEEKS AND NO ONE EVER WILL.

Oh, this is actually getting rough, you guys. I mean, put that all-caps on a T-shirt—both sides—but I'm starting to be truly embarrassed.

I'LL BE THE WORLD'S OLDEST VIRGIN, AND THE WORLD'S BIGGEST LOSER WHO NEVER HAD ANYONE TELL HER THAT HE LOVED HER AND MEANT IT. Okay? I've said it. There. It's out. And from what I've heard about what's-his-face, I'm just going to end up liking the guy, maybe end up loving the guy, and then be screwed over. Again.

I'm developing a very negative attitude towards men in general. I think that this is not good. I mean the only guys that I care about in this whole fucking world are [HOLLY HUNTER BOY], [HOMEROOM BOY], and you.

Yes. Yes, I did. Yes, I did just slaughter a quote from *Some Kind of Wonderful* and yes I did think of myself as Mary Stuart Masterson's character without the drums. BOYS WERE MY DRUMS. You guys. Boys were my drums. (And books.)
I apologize in advance for this next section.

And I've fallen in love with all three of them and all three of them have called me the "F" word. I'm a friend. I've memorized the fucking speech.

"Oh, I really like you and everything, but I think that, oh, um…God, this is hard, uh…fuck. I feel like a dick. See, I like you. I like you a lot, don't get me wrong. Oh…shit. See, I like you too much. Do you understand? I-think-that-this-is-moving-too-fast-and-I'd-like-to-just-be-friends. Oh, did I hurt you? Oh, shit. The last thing I'd ever want to do is hurt you. Believe me. I feel like a dick. I'm sorry. Are you okay? Dude, are you crying? Because, don't, man, I'm not worth it. I'm not worth this. I'm scum. I'm a dick. I'm sorry. Are you still my buddy?"

I am now one hundred percent positive that I gave a print-out (A PRINT-OUT!) of this letter to this boy, who said some version of this speech to me, albeit in probably an even more awkward way, as an attempt to let him know…what, that he hurt me? As if he's still reading at this point. WE ARE ON PAGE THREE.

Oh, God, you guys. This next part. It's amazing.

> Yeah, your fucking buddy till the fucking end of time, that's me. Just call me Fred. We'll get together on Friday's sometime (if you aren't too busy with some real girl, that is) and we'll go bowling, down a couple of brewski's, pick up a couple of cutsey dames, treat them like shit, pick our asses, watch a football game, eat until we puke, light our farts, take a shit, you know, buddy stuff. Yep that's me, old buddy, old pal. [*sic*] [*sic*] [*sic*]

"Cutsey dames"!!!

(Ass-picking and fart-lighting aside, it's not really that bad of night. Fred sounds like fun.)

> I really don't think that this is worth it anymore, all of this love shit. Love sucks. It's hurts. [*sic*] It rips out everything inside you, sticks it in a blender on puree, and then shoves the bloody massive pulp back inside your soul to just sit there and rot. Love sucks, and I'm not going to take it anymore. I'm giving up guys—I know I've said it before, I said it to [K] many times, but this time, I'm going to do it. I'm man-free. Ice Pam.

Yes. Yes, I did. Yes, I did just slaughter a Lloyd Dobler quote from *Say Anything*…And yes, I think you're right, there was also some kind of attempt at a quote from *Network*. Can you feel my pain NOW?!

> Nothing can penetrate this heart. Not all of the roses in the world. Not all of the bottles of rain. Not for all of the kisses, not for all of the sweet nothings, not for all of the "I love you"s that one can say in a lifetime. It probably could feel worse than this and I don't want to risk that chance, so if I just stop it now and say fuck it all, then maybe I'll spare myself some pain. I doubt it, because right about now I feel like someone has placed

my insides on hot coals, and my stomach is desparately [*sic*] trying to jump off. No, I feel fine. No, I feel fucking great. I could live without guys. Who needs them? Men, shmen.

This girl has lost her hormonal mind. Oh, my God. She clearly drank way too many bottles of rain.

None of them really care about me, anyway. Yeah, I'm sure of it. Definately. [*sic*] Yep. Uh-huh...Boy it's lonely being guyless.

WHAT AM I DOING? I sent this to someone! Someone read this! This is insanity.

But that's okay, because I'm ICE PAM. Heart of ice. Soul stone cold. I will never melt again. Don't look at me like that, you know what those puppy-dog eyes do to me.

WHO AM I TALKING TO? WHY IS FIFTEEN SO STUPID?

Ah, but not anymore, not ICE PAM. I'm impermeable. Not even you will make me like guys. Nope. Not gonna do it.

Little Pam Life Lesson #43: When writing a love letter discussing whether or not you will ever find someone who will love you longer than two weeks so that you can lose your virginity to someone who respects you enough to wait for that all-important third week, it's best to close your multiple-personality rants with a well-known *SNL* catchphrase coined by Dana Carvey with his George H. W. Bush impersonation.
Fucking. DORK.

Maybe this new outlook on guys would be a lot easier if I convinced myself a little more. This should be easy. Hold on, let me slap myself (I don't bruise when I do it).

Super Mario Brothers Boy had a thing about giving me bruises, because it takes so little for me to get one. For *years*. He never slapped me, or did something to intentionally make me suffer. It took only the slightest poke to make me bruise. And okay, sometimes he'd bite me, but I'd allow it because it meant his actual mouth was on my actual body. I really do bruise easily. In fact, I have one on my wrist right now, from this past Monday, when I foolishly and recklessly decided to open a door. The door didn't close on me. I opened it. And hurt myself. Do you know how *hard* that is to do?

And yes, I know that people say "I hurt myself on a door" when it's a cry for help that they're being abused, but in this case I really am in an abusive relationship with entrances and exits. Doors literally hit me on the ass on my way out, and they always have.

Look how [HOLLY HUNTER BOY] treated you.
Look how [OMITTED] treated you, he left you for [ANOTHER GIRL] during the course of *Dick Tracy*.

Until this moment, I believe I had successfully blocked that out of my memory. It's back now. And at least now I understand why I remember seeing that movie in a theater, but have absolutely no recollection of a single minute of it. I don't even remember who Dick Tracy Boy was. I cannot picture his face. I'd explain precisely how a fifteen-year-old girl gets left for another girl during a 7:00 P.M. screening of a Warren Beatty/Madonna film, but I think whatever pathetic teen tragedy you could imagine will be close to accurate, if not exactly what happened. What a sad pattern of boy-related things happening to LP during screenings of movies. I still break out in hives whenever someone mentions *House Party 2*. (It happens more often than you'd think.)

WAIT. I remember. It's the rhyming name kid I mentioned earlier in this letter. He's the one who left me during *Dick Tracy*. He and his long-term girlfriend broke up and he started dating me, but then he asked me not to tell anyone we were dating, and then we walked past his ex-girlfriend in the cafeteria, and that's when he held my hand, and the next thing I knew his ex-girlfriend was dating Super Mario Brothers Boy (which broke my heart and must be why I'm mentioning it here), and then Rhyming Name Boy found out and asked me why my friend was dating his ex-girlfriend and OH GOD I AM REMEMBERING THIS IN REAL TIME RIGHT NOW AS I TYPE THIS he asked me to set up a double date, so we all went to see *Dick Tracy* and during the movie he just started making out with his ex, Super Mario Brothers Boy and I on either side.

HIGH SCHOOL SUCKS.

Oh, man. I should have kept that blocked out! Because what's worse is like, three years later I saw him at a Denny's and he straight-up pretended he had never met me before. "I bet his tongue remembers me," I muttered to the person I was sitting with at the counter. But I didn't say it to him. I said nothing to him and his stupid rhyming name. Ironically, the guy I was sitting with at the Denny's counter would go on to secret-date me in an effort to get back at his ex-girlfriend.

JUST AFTER HIGH SCHOOL SUCKS, TOO.

Look how [THIRTY-SIX HOURS BOY] treated you—23 hours before he wanted to be your buddy. Look how [SCHOOL BUS BOY] treated you—you were only one of three that weekend and he at least wrote letters to the other two...true they were the exact same letters, but at least he thought of them afterwards.

Yeah, I didn't get over it easily.

Look how [HOMEROOM BOY] dropped you before you even got to do anything with him. Look how [BOY I'M WRITING THIS LETTER TO BUT FOR SOME REASON I PUT HIS NAME HERE SO THAT I'M TALKING ABOUT HIM TO HIM. I AM A MASSIVE DORK.] changed his mind for reasons you still don't understand. And if you don't stop this bullshit soon, you are going to be singing the same song about [TACO BELL BOY].

I'm sorry I'm going on about this. Probably either boring you or pissing you off.

And if that line doesn't give you flashbacks to your own high school notes, I don't know what will.

This just isn't the kind of thing I'd talk to [K] about because she says, "Cheer up, Pamie." because she's in love and making me sick. Since you probably won't talk to me at all about it because you never seem to talk about my serious notes, I assume you are just going to do the same, kind of act like you read a story or something. Well, it's not a story, dammit. These are my feelings, here is my soul, pitifully dripping off of the pages of this disgustingly stupid and boring letter. And I only wrote it because I need your help.

Pam

I do realize that in this letter I told you that I love you, but I pretty much consider that subject an entirely different letter.

And...SCENE!

How about that ending, folks, huh? You got to admit, that totally surprised you. Oh, that makes me laugh every time I read it. What a postscript.

I have to admit, I am not sure what kind of help LP is asking for. Advice on Taco Bell Boy? A volunteer to take her virginity? An admission of love? Someone to talk her out of giving up on men?

What does eventually happen is Super Mario Brothers Boy finds out I once wrote a 200-page letter to Holly Hunter Boy and demands I write him one that is 205 pages long. "I mean, unless he's more important to you than I am."

Two days later, I delivered 205 pages, straight to his face.

But this letter I just shared, this is a *mother* of a letter. I really wish I could say it was unsent. I do. But I just don't think it was. I bet I waited days for him to write back or call or something, and he probably never did. Most likely he didn't even read it, because who would read that craziness? I'd be like, "*Oh, that letter? Uh, yeah, it got taken up by the bus driver and she threw it away.*"

Which is why I was all crafty. "Oh, no problem! I SAVED IT TO MY HARD DRIVE. Here is another copy! W.B.S.! Lylas! But not really, because I love you like a soul mate! So, it's really more Lylasm!"

(My own editor drew a big ol' circle around 'LYLAS' in this manuscript, which means she's too young to know what LYLAS is. I'm worried girls no longer sign their letters with the most important sign-off from my youth. LYLAS. It means "Love You Like A Sister." Learn it. Live it. Love it. Text it. It's so much better than that flaming poo emoji.)

I'm so glad I'm not fifteen anymore. I hope you're not fifteen anymore. I'm glad boys aren't fifteen anymore. Sure, there are times when we regress back into our sophomore-year selves, but isn't it better now, when we have cars that we can drive away in, and money we can spend to get on planes to go far, far away, and like, not just a room, but our own *homes*? We can slam that front door and write in our diaries and do whatever we want because nobody can ground us anymore.

Nobody can ground us anymore!

Shit, that reminds me. I've got a traffic ticket I need to pay.

How To Lose A Girl In One Day

You may have noticed the part where I breezed past being in a supply closet with K's sort-of-boyfriend in a movie theatre without mentioning for a second that perhaps I have no business being anywhere near that guy's Coke bottle.

I'm coming back to that now. K deserves her own chapter.

I met her in English class freshman year, where she sat in the back corner. I don't know if it was an alphabetical thing or by choice, but the back corner was where K would have chosen to be. That way she could keep an eye on everyone.

She had short, dark hair cut in an asymmetrical bob that swayed and bounced around her face. She wore heavy eyeliner and red lipstick. I'd never seen anyone wear that much foundation and powder, patting and layering makeup until you could no longer determine her natural skin color, which was a lovely olive. She was short, top-heavy, and wore the shortest mini-skirts over fishnets and zippered boots.

She was the coolest girl I'd ever met. And for some reason, she wanted to be my friend. Maybe at first it was because we were neighbors who rode the same bus and got off at the same stop. But I think she was just a nice enough person that she found my dorky awkwardness endearing. It let her be just as bizarre.

We were kindred spirits, and I'm so lucky to have met her.

She got to decorate her room however she wanted. This means she painted her walls green before hand-painting swirling designs in white. She made a collage of an eyeball out of magazine clippings of eyeballs. It hung next to her poster from *Taxi Driver*. Her ceiling was decorated in used chewing gum. *Our* used chewing gum. We'd buy a pack of something pink and chomp it with gusto before jamming it into her popcorn ceiling. Sometimes we'd squish out initials, sometimes a peace sign. I can no longer remember which one of us did the Red Hot Chili Peppers symbol. I'd like to think we did it together.

K loved music and fashion and being punk rock. She was the VIP that got me past the velvet rope and into a new world, one where I finally felt like I belonged. I was so much more comfortable around the self-proclaimed weirdos and outcasts. Here were the people who would dork out over a Beastie Boys album or want to spend an entire evening dipping their hair in Kool-Aid. Nobody thought it was strange that I wore polka dot boxers under my enormous jeans and an oversized shirt for *Phantom of the Opera* (I've never seen it, nor could I recognize one song, but that shirt was glow-in-the-dark and I loved it). I was walking around like the most uncool version of Left-Eye, and yet this new group of friends would just say, "Cool Docs." And I knew they were right, because all Doc Martens were cool.

It was the closest I ever got to cool, even though I was doing it so weirdly.

I was finally around other people who had parents who both worked, who read books nobody else wanted to read, who liked skateboarding and indie movies. People who had heard of Monty Python! People who knew who The Outsiders were! People who got excited to go to the museum—the Contemporary Arts Museum! The one with the weird art!

There were all kinds of new people, but mostly there were new boys. The other girls didn't like me as much as K did. They looked at me with a side-eye because I was different and a little shy around them. Girls always could make me quieter. With boys, it was always simpler, easier. You just talked about stuff. And by that I mean tangible stuff. Things. Boys talk about things. Girls talk about things you cannot see. Feelings. Gossip. Mind games. I did not know how to do any of that.

I got closer to the boys, and soon that meant I was standing so close to them they started to see me. I wasn't thinking I was stealing boyfriends. I wasn't thinking I was pursuing someone who belonged to someone else. I always saw myself as a sidekick, someone unseeable.

But eventually some boy would see me, probably because I was ALWAYS THERE and so clearly available emotionally and physically that he had no choice but to wonder, "Maybe this girl, then." Then I'd be so surprised that I got his attention, I wasn't respectful of his relationship. I didn't know how to maneuver around a boundary. I'd never had a boundary with a boy. I mean, not one that wasn't a full-on fence or brick wall he'd put up to keep me away.

I just couldn't see how sometimes getting kissed didn't mean I'd won something. Even though I wasn't ugly, it still always seemed next to impossible that someone would want me. Every single kiss was a new validation that I was worth being chosen.

So when I found myself in a supply closet with a boy who was technically maybe supposed to be K's boyfriend, I didn't think to stop and say, "No." I didn't think about it, because I was still trying to figure out how I got in there in the first place. Why me? It never occurred to me that some boys just grab whatever's closest. I kept trying to find the story in it, to figure out what was special.

I guess I can rationalize that since I moved a lot growing up, I hadn't gotten used to the concept of people sticking around. For my entire life, a friend that day was gone in a few months. But I wish I'd known then how selfish it was, what I was doing. I wish I had seen what it looked like to everyone else, to anyone who didn't know me, and to the ones who knew me best. I was so busy thinking about the start of a relationship, I couldn't see all the ones I was destroying.

The first time it happened, after 2 Live Crew Boy told everyone I was crying before he got my shirt off, the girls were so mean to me, especially the ones close with his girlfriend. I just assumed *women be bitches.* I only dated that guy for a week before he broke up with me. I was the one who got hurt in that situation, or so I thought.

I never told K about the supply closet. When Coke Bottle took her away during the movie, I knew I'd done something that would hurt her feelings. I hated how I couldn't tell her what an asshole the guy was she was with, how he didn't care about her enough to leave me alone, but I felt like there was no way I could tell her what happened without coming across as just as bad. So yeah, I did know what I'd done was wrong. I just didn't want it to be.

Then there was the one who would go on to become my first real boyfriend. He was dating K when we became friends, but she had an early phone curfew. When he got off the phone with her, he'd call me. I'm sure I thought it was harmless, him quietly listening while I went on and on about absolutely nothing.

But then that boy chose me. One day he chose me. Not her.

I rationalized it again. This was a real relationship, I told myself. This was going to last longer than hers did. Besides, her mother didn't want her dating him. I thought everybody's anger toward our relationship only validated it. It made me fight for it even harder. How romantic it was, two against the world.

But it was a mistake. It was wrong.

I lost her, and it's one of my life's biggest regrets.

Over the years I've tried to find her, but she's not on any social media. I've seen pictures from other friends, heard stories about her life and how she was doing, but there wasn't a way to directly contact her. I didn't know if she thought of me like I'd thought of her, if she missed me the way I missed her.

I thought of her often, especially when I was in college, even more so as I found more people who would've loved her sense of humor, her style and grace. It was an incredibly long time before I made a close female friend again, and really, I've never had a girlfriend like that, one I saw every day. K and I shared clothes, money, food. We once went on a diet together where one couldn't eat without the other's permission. We made stupid videos and art projects and went shopping together. We did nothing together, all the time. If only I could've known how special that was, back when I had it. I tossed it away to be chosen by a boy before I'd know how rare it was to be chosen by someone like her.

I wish I could say I learned from that mistake, and never made friends with a boy who was taken, but I would be lying. I would be rationalizing yet again. I never actively tried to steal someone's boyfriend away, but I knew how to wear people down until I was the only one left standing. I knew how to keep someone's attention.

I once said to my husband, "We never had to do that awkward finding-excuses-to-touch-each-other part of our relationship. You know, where we're just testing out friendship and maybe we're both involved with someone else and we are realizing there might be something more."

He looked at me like I had just shaved my head. "That's because we're grown-ups who act grown. We didn't have to hurt anybody to find each other."

I owe a lot of apologies for the road map my heart has taken.

I was in Austin on my last book tour reading from a chapter about two best friends when I looked out at the audience and saw K. There she was, sitting in front of me, and I had to stop talking or I was going to break down into the Ugly Cry.

After the reading I finally got a chance to hug her. I cried and told her how much I've always missed her. I told her how much I've thought about her, how I'd tried to find her, how important she was to me, and still is. How I wouldn't be the person I am without her, and how grateful I am for her.

But I don't know if I ever apologized. It never seemed like the right situation to bring up the past like that. "*Hi, how's your sister? Your parents? I'm sorry I stole your boyfriend in the tenth grade. Can I get you a beer? I still think about that time you had an iguana.*"

The truth is, I don't know if I could ever apologize enough. I don't mean about the boy, because that's not the worst thing I did. The worst thing is that when I lost her, I didn't fight with everything I had to get her back. I let her go. I let her disappear. I'll never be able to forgive myself for wasting all of that time. Time I could've had knowing her.

Here I Go Again...

It starts at my face. This warm rush trickles to my cheeks and a redness forms. The rush dances—tingling down my spine, following my veins to the tips of my fingers and swirling at the pit of my stomach—making me feel as queasy as that time we rode that roller coaster seven times in a row. My legs go next, feeling like they are caving in and they lose all stability as my toes go numb from anxiety. My hair is standing on end and my fists are clenched and I'm biting my tongue.

You must be nearby.

Dear Dorkhouse Forum

The following might be the most embarrassing non-letter thing I wrote my fifteenth year. There's a kind of sweetness to it, as it was from the last time in my life that I was this exact combination of shy and secretly not shy.

> I did not want to go to this family reunion. In my opinion, my entire family is completely and totally crazy. But, I was 24, and I looked forward to the freezing temperatures of Connecticut in December, hobnobbing with total lunatics. But, I'm wierd [*sic*], and I decide to go.

Didn't "24" seem so grown-up at fifteen?

> So I'm standing here, listening to my aunt telling me how big I've gotten, and I begin to realize that there are a lot of people here I have never seen before. I told my aunt that I was thirsty and left her jabbering to my sister about how big she's gotten.

> As I stand over the punch bowl, I notice that someone is beginning to get himself a drink as well. I always notice hands first (and that's probably why I learned palm reading)—

Shut up. You know you want me to tell you about your lifeline. And I'll do it, too, because I can't stop myself. But I can't do it right now. There's too many of you, and we have a lot of letters to get through.

Okay, just one. Look at your left palm. Now rotate your wrist so you're looking at the side of your hand, just below your pinkie. In the space between the crevices made by your pinkie and the first main line that cuts across your palm (your heart line), you'll see some tiny creases. Count them. That's how many kids you're supposed to have.

You're welcome.

If you're wondering the name of your future spouse, go get an apple, take the stem in between your thumb and forefinger and start reciting the alphabet, twisting the apple with each letter. Whichever letter you're on when the stem breaks, that's the first letter of the name of your future love. (Good luck to all of you crushing on Zacharys and Zoes, hoping your apple stem will make it through twenty-five rotations.)

I'm stalling because I know you're about to read this next paragraph.

> —and I notice that this guy has got great hands. So, I slowly look up from his hands. He's wearing a T-shirt that says "Free Nelson Mandela" and a suede jacket over it. Then I see his face. Even though he had on a baseball cap and sunglasses, one look at those cheekbones and I knew who I was staring at.

> Johnny Depp.

The thing is…okay. Okay, I'll wait for you to stop laughing. No, no, it's okay. Go ahead. The thing is…oh, you're still laughing.

> He smiled at me, just like the millions of smiles I have posted all around my room of him. My heart was racing ninety to nothing, and I knew I was shaking, but I tried desperately to keep my cool.

Dear Dorkhouse Forum. I swear every word of this is untrue. Please enjoy my fanfic to myself about meeting my celebrity crush. At a FAMILY REUNION. Which I'm sure says so much about my relationship issues and how I felt about moving a lot and isolation and confusion over exactly what kind of role a man is supposed to have in my life, and what it means to feel like you need a hero to rescue you all the time, particularly when dealing with your family.

> "Hi," he said, in the way that only he could. I know I was staring, and that my mouth was a little open, but it's not every day that you see the hunk of your dreams standing right in front of you.

I feel like this might be the only time in my entire life I use the word "hunk." I hope that's true.

> "Hi," I said, breathlessly. "You know, you might be able to fool everyone else here with that sunglasses and hat getup, but you can't fool me."

> He raised one finger to his lips to silence me, and I told him that I wouldn't tell.

In my memory over the years, this story has changed. I thought I set this in a flea market, for example. I thought he was wearing that floppy hat he often wears, and that it was sunny outside, and we were leaning over a table covered in necklaces. I thought I was supposed to be younger than twenty-four (Because it says in here that my room was covered in his posters. At twenty-four?), and that he was checking me out, which was why we started talking in the first place. What if I remember it that way because there's a *second* version of this story that I wrote somewhere, but gave away?

> "Why are you at a family reunion if you don't want to be seen?" I asked him, and I wondered how in the world could this guy be related to me.

> "My mom told me I had no choice. What's your name?"

> "Oh, I'm sorry, Pam. Pam Ribon." We shook hands.

> "Pleased to meet you, are you a Pam or a Pamela?"

"Pamela. But no one calls me that."

"Then that's what I'll call you. Are you sure you're related to me? No one in my family is as georgeous [*sic*] as you."

I could feel myself blush as I said, "Everyone in my family that I know of is crazy."

He laughed and said, "Then we must be related. Come on, let's go check the chart."

In the middle of the whole family reunion fiasco is a huge chart, telling the family tree.

"I don't understand how we can be related," I said. "I mean, you're part Cherokee, and I'm Polish and Czech."

"See," he said pointing a finger to a name, "your great aunt married one of my great uncles, somehow that made us one, two, three, four, five, six, seven, eight, ninth cousins twice removed."

"Wow," I said, because I couldn't think of anything else to say.

"But," he said, "that makes us so far apart that it's like we aren't related at all."

"Oh."

"But that's good, isn't it?"

I looked up into his eyes (he had taken off his sunglasses) and stared into the depths of his big brown eyes. I could get used to this.

"Yeah," I said. "That's good."

"You want to get out of here?"

"I thought you'd never ask."

We left in his blue BMW, listening to the radio. I couldn't help but sneak looks at this great looking person sitting beside me. God if this was a dream, I don't ever want to wake up.

To Be Continued…

I am sure I am not alone in my disappointment when I say that this story is never continued.

The BMW is the best part. This was a grown-up conversation! This was how you met a boy and fell in love. You went to a family reunion but acted older and saner than everyone else, and then the celebrity with the fancy car would whisk you away before he even told you his middle name. (Just kidding, he didn't have to. It's Christopher. John Christopher Depp II. I kind of know a lot about him.)

I'm just glad it's legal for ninth cousins twice removed to have hot sex, or Little Pam would have been so sad.

(I'm Guessing Nobody Asked Me For This)

You ask for gifts of written words. A simple request, I know. I grasp pen in hand and fall speechless, my ink well dries. I find it difficult to summarize love in prose; poetry leaves emotions too vague. It seems that the stronger my feelings grow, the harder it is to symbolize them with words. They sound cheap and trite. You deserve better.

I know I love you when I am convinced I see patterns in clouds forming your name. I hear the raindrops pattering a love song I dedicate only to you (my heartbeat knows the song well; it plays it often when you are near). My dreams consist of a paradise lost with you, a little house in the middle of a field, our only neighbors are a family of rabbits. The sight and smell of flowers reminds me of your smile. I am convinced I hear your name constantly, when oftentimes it is only the wind, murmuring contently as the sun engulfs me in a warmth comparable only to your embrace. Music is no masterpiece compared to the sound of your voice filling my ears. Books hold me no prisoner—your conversation is all I need. I feed off your love, drink from the pure happiness you fill me with. I am drunk from the esctacy [sic] of our perfection. I live and breathe for you. My heart beats for you. My only hope is that one day we will entwine our bodies in a promise and never again feel the yearning the word "goodbye" creates. I love you.

If I could harness the fire in the world in a kiss, I would deliver it to you. I want to shower you with all of the clear blue rain this earth creates.

I want to sprinkle snowflakes on your tongue. I want to paint your room a sunrise, and tuck you in with a sunset. I want to capture nature's elements and store them in a box for your leisure.

I want you trapped in my basement where I clothe you in "elements" and force you to eat snow.

You deserve all the best things this world has to offer.

I'm Only Sleeping (Or Am I?)

Super Mario Brothers Boy and I had the kind of relationship where I always assumed one day he'd turn to me, take my hand, get all misty and say, "It was you. All along, it was you." It was more than just how we fought like hormone-crazed, teenaged siblings or how we chose to spend our days after school together. It wasn't just in our romantic meet-cute in that we were on the same bus route. It was in how we were linked. At the risk of sounding like my younger self, all the tiny ways our lives connected felt like one big, important story. Like the first time I ever had him over for dinner.

I can't remember if my parents just finally wanted to meet the boy they knew was in their house every day after school while they were both at work or if I insisted on having him over for dinner so that I got an extra hour or two of his time. It couldn't have been that I *wanted* him to have dinner with my family, because I tried to avoid anybody meeting my father for any extended period of time. There was the very real chance that he'd flat-out ask Super Mario Brothers Boy if he had any intentions of moving past Vaselinesturbation to sliding directly into his daughter's vagina.

Add to my father's tendency for unpredictable straight talk the fact that Super Mario Brothers Boy loved crossing the line. You gave him an authority figure or a boundary, and he'd find a way to challenge it. He was almost always serving some sort of detention or in-school suspension. The two hundred and five page note was a request from him; an inmate asking for a box of books. I know in my weird, young head I was scribbling the closest thing to a conjugal visit I could deliver, straight to his lonely asylum located between the Yearbook staff and the special needs kids. Yeah, that's right. I word-fucked his eyes *hard*, people. I gave him so much paragraph!

SMB Boy knew all my secrets, not just because he spent so much time with me, but because I wanted someone who was going to be with me for the rest of my life to know all my secrets. This means he knew some of the extreme choices that had been made by my father to punish me.

One Saturday morning, back when I was in junior high, my father discovered I'd ditched cleaning the litter box for yet another day. Instead of grounding me, he forbade me from using the bathroom for the entire weekend. *"Now you'll know how the cat feels,"* he said. My choices were: find somewhere else to pee or go in the backyard. I spent most of the next two days frantically riding my ten-speed over to my friend Tamara's house. She lived a mile away and had a big, fun family who enjoyed my company. I remember one time I was anxiously pedaling up to her house, legs as pressed together at the thighs as I could manage while still balancing a bike, when I spotted Tamara's mother already at the front door, holding it wide, waving her arm at me like an encouraging spectator on the sidelines of a marathon.

"Here she comes!" she whooped. *"Get that potty ready for her!"*

I was lucky to have Tamara's family when I got grounded from the bathroom. Unfortunately they weren't around when I was grounded from fluids (I'd failed to drink all my milk at breakfast), sleep (woke Dad up because I was talking on the phone past my phone curfew), or food (had gained too much weight and was no longer trusted to eat at non-monitored times).

SMB Boy couldn't stand it. "Your family makes me crazy," he said. "Just go to sleep. How can they make you not sleep?"

"Dad sat me on a chair and he watched me."

"I guess it could be worse," he said. "I know a girl who wasn't allowed to go trick-or-treating this year because her parents said she and her sister aren't allowed to eat any candy because they're too fat."

"That was *me*. I told you that."

"Your family drives me crazy!"

So one night SMB Boy is sitting next to my dad at the dinner table and it's that awkward kind of quiet that only happened when my family sat down to eat. Dad started in on some small talk, asking SMB Boy what his father did for a living.

Our fathers were both in hotel management. I've never known anybody else who had a parent in hotel management.

Dad asked SMB Boy if he knew his father. "No, I don't think so," SMB Boy said. "He lives in New York."

"How come your parents are divorced?"

Dad's direct question was met with SMB Boy's direct answer.

"My father tried to run his family like he ran his hotel," he said. "But your family isn't supposed to be treated like employees. You can't just tell them what to do and they have to do it."

There has never been a silence on this planet as heavy and thick and terrifying as the silence that followed that moment. I remember looking across the table and seeing my younger sister's mouth in this tiny, tight "o," her eyes lemur-wide. My mother's heartbeat became audible, thumping something that sounded an awful lot like, "*Ohshit. Ohshit. Ohshit. Ohshit.*"

Then my father said a man's name. "That's what you said his name is, right? Your father?"

"That is his name," SMB Boy said. "But I didn't tell you that."

"Oh. Then I guess I must have met him at some point somewhere."

Dad went back to eating, my mother's heartbeat quieted, and my sister went back to her dinner, visibly relieved there was no further confrontation.

But underneath the table, I grabbed SMB Boy's hand and squeezed the most heartfelt thank you.

I tell you that story so that you understand why I would find myself continuing to pine for SMB Boy even when all signs pointed to the fact that we were not going to get together. Like, ever. We were never going to get together.

Except that we might. It always seemed like we might. I was Charlie Brown, and SMB Boy's commitment was the football, no doubt.

There was the night we made out and then he called me an hour after I got home to express his deep regrets, to take it all back and declare it a huge mistake. "I don't want to lose you," he said, to which I wailed, "*How can you lose me when you won't have me?*"

I fully admit I was exhausting. I don't know why nobody used that exact word. "*You are exhausting,*" someone should have said to me. "*And I can't imagine how much more prolific you would be if you had access to a computer.*"

Making out followed by take-backs became a running theme in my relationship with SMB Boy. I thought maybe he kept wanting to test it out. Make sure I was really the girl he wanted to kiss. I believed him when he said he was worried he'd ruin our friendship. How could I not fall for that sentence? It sounded like it was ripped from LP's own journal.

Then there was the night SMB Boy and I made out on his couch, but he later claimed he did not remember any of it because—*get this*—he was asleep.

"You were asleep."

"Yeah, I guess. I mean, did something happen?"

"Yes. For about half an hour."

"No. I'm pretty sure I was asleep."

"Your hands weren't asleep."

"Honestly, Pam, I don't know what you're talking about."

"You should see a doctor, or something. For this condition where you make out with girls in your sleep because I think it could get you arrested someday."

And then I went and wrote this:

2 / March / 1991

I've got to learn to close that door. I need to teach myself to shut and lock that part of my mind that constantly screams your name. It screams and screams until the echos [sic] fill my head and I can't think of anyone or anything else. The only time the screams are quieted is when I am near you, and then the screams turn into these subliminal whispers, bouncing in my head and filling my mind with images and scenarios that involve you and me and an undying passion that you read about in romance novels. I need to silence the scream, end the agony. I need to bolt up that door and shut up those pleas for you. Because I want to go on living. And I sure as hell can't as long as the desire for you still has the power to rule my mind.

By closing this door I hope to end a lot more than sorrows. I hope I'll end my worries, my anger and frustrations, and to end my confusion. Slamming this door shut will cease my yearning for your touch, my desire for your kiss. Closing this door will make me stand on my own—for once. It will make me be myself again. It might make me happy again—in time.

God, you can tell I'm so *impressed* with myself.

In the end, I'm glad I had the sleepmacking experience with SMB Boy because it prepared me for the next time someone tried this move.

Yeah, that's right. I've had MORE THAN ONE BOY claim to be asleep while also trying to mess around with me. With SMB Boy, I was so in love I would have pretended to be asleep just to have him near me. *Sleeping: the only time I'm not capable of writing and delivering a love letter.*

When the second boy tried to fool around with me while actively feigning sleep (eyes closed, heavy limbs, slight snoring sound while trying to slip his tongue in my ear), I did what I should have done to SMB Boy.

I kicked him in the nards.

And you guys, I have to tell you: it felt really good.

"I had to do it," I told him. "You were asleep and trying to fool around with me. I was helping you wake up."

…I probably didn't say that. I probably went home and wrote something just like this:

3, March, 1991

Life confuses me. Life is like the biggest poser in the world. It acts like it's this big deal—it's the coolest. It's the best. So you want to be friends with it, get closer to it, so it makes you cool too. You seize life with both hands, expecting it to be this enormous rush and this overwhelming feeling of happiness and you expect the coolness to start to rub off on you. You stick with this new buddy for a while—maybe even years—but it seems the longer you hang around, the more fake and superficial it seems. It's all about status, and who looks superior to whom, and you realize that there are more important things to do. But still, you figure that life is just going through some sort of phase and you continue to link arms with it. After a while, life starts to lose its appeal. You've stripped away the superficiality and you find that it is really dull and boring and not much to it.

Life. It's pretty much bullshit. Brought to you by the number fifteen.

There was a third time in my life when sleep factored heavily into my heavy petting, but this time both of us were right where we wanted to be, and nobody was faking slumber during the make out session.

It was my sweetest high school romance. If there was a boy I dated in high school who was the most like me when it came down to innocence and optimistic naïveté, it was this boy. We were silly and played games and drew pictures and watched sunsets and had a romance that could have been created by a five-year-old with a box of glitter.

We dated long enough that his mother bought him a box of condoms to keep in his bathroom. I still haven't emotionally recovered. She thought I was a whore who had sex with her son! I didn't! We didn't! I swear!

(In case you're reading this, Mom of Nice Boy: I'm sorry about that time you found me naked in your hot tub. Only now am I able to handle how freaking funny it is that you proceeded to hold a twenty-minute conversation standing over me while we both pretended nothing was wrong.)

So Nice Boy and I were seventeen and we decided one night to go out to this lonely road and look at the stars. (See? We were adorable!) I mean, maybe we also knew we were going to make out, but at the time we said we were going to look at the stars. The point is, the street was always dead and it was one of those Texas farm roads that look depressingly barren during the day, but at night the skies explode in thick, shiny stars, heavy with romance.

So there we were, looking at the stars and dancing to The Doors, because that's what all boys liked to do that year. This was back when Val Kilmer was hot. We were under this big, bright moon when we started in on some serious first-to-second-base action. We're kissing in the backseat. I would tell you what kind of car it was but I truly don't know a thing about cars. This one might have been blue, I think. Or silver. Cars never mattered to me. It was only awesome if you had one.

Back to the make out. I've got my shirt off and I'm in my bra. Just as I pull off his shirt, headlights blast through the foggy windows.

Someone was driving toward us.

Nice Boy yells, "Get down!"

Was he trying to protect me from rapists? Serial killers? Roaming packs of parents? The sex police? I don't know, but I was just as terrified.

We hunkered down together, our semi-naked bodies clutched in a state of suspended anxiety as the headlights passed us. We peeked out the back window to watch the rear lights grow smaller.

But then that car slowed down.

And then it stopped.

"I think he saw us," I aptly remarked.

"Is it a cop?"

"I can't see through the windows so well."

"Is it a cop?!"

Terror like I was wearing a bra made out of cocaine and he was scooping meth off my thighs. Like we were sitting on bank-robbed cash and our legs were stolen weapons. "It's backing up! It's backing up! It's backing up!"

"Is it a cop? Is it a cop? Is it a cop?"

Never a worry that it's a madman or a rapist. Just the cops, ready to arrest us for…I guess for being *so damn sexy* in public.

Anyway, it was totally a cop.

We jumped into the front seat of the car. I was fumbling with my shirt, unable to button the front while re-fastening my bra in the back. I had too many fingers and not enough arms!

As the officer approached, I knew I didn't have enough time to get all of my clothes back on. Nice Boy quickly fastened his seatbelt just as I came up with the perfect solution.

"Tell him I'm sleeping!"

"*What*?!"

I'm reclining the seat, hissing in the dark. "Tell him I'm asleep and that you don't want to wake me up but you pulled over to check on me!"

"You really think he's going to believe that?"

"I don't think we have a choice! We're screwed! We're so screwed!"

I am not exaggerating the drama that was going on inside that Grand Am. (I don't know if it was a Grand Am. It could've been a Grand Prix. I'm sure one of those cars doesn't have a backseat, anyway. Cars are so boring unless you're in a Johnny Depp BMW.)

"Don't you think he's going to ask why I took off your shirt while you were sleeping?"

"Tell him I was hot or something! Stop talking to me! I'm asleep!"

I'm reclined in the passenger seat with my shirt thrown over my chest while my topless boyfriend sits in the passenger side pulling out his registration. This is what the policeman saw when he knocked on the window.

"Hello, Officer."

"Would you please step out of the vehicle?"

"Of course, yes, that makes sense, yes. I'm doing that right now. She's asleep."

He said that at the exact same time I asked, "Do you want me to step out of the car, too?"

"No, Miss. Why don't you just concentrate on putting your clothes back on."

"Okay, Officer, I will do that."

"Thank you, Miss."

"I was hot."

"Alright, then."

"I mean, the temperature. I was hot. Not that I was attractive."

"Okay, I'm just going to step to the back of the vehicle with the driver, here."

I sat in the front seat, completely freaking out. Through the side view mirror I could see the officer reading Nice Boy's license. Nice Boy was completely Farley-ing out, slapping his head, jerking his body. "*This was so stupid! Stupid! Stupid!*"

The officer walked back to me and leaned in through the driver's side window.

"What's your name?" he asked.

Please don't call my parents, please don't call my parents, please don't call my—

"Please don't call my parents."

"Your name."

"Pam."

"And how old are you?"

Don't tell him you're a minor. There's probably a city-wide curfew here. This is some Footloose *shit and you don't want it. But then he'll ask for your license and you'll get busted and go to jail for lying to the cops and then you'll be so grounded. You'd better tell him the truth. Tell him you're seventeen before you're in any more trouble.*

"I'm eighteen."

Oh, my God we are going to jail and we are so busted and why aren't you still pretending to be asleep? Why do you like to watch stars and sunsets with this boy? When will you get in trouble for actually having sex? What is wrong with you?

"And are you here completely of your own will?"

Wait. Hold up. Think that one out before you answer it. Which answer gets you less grounded? Nice Boy would totally take the heat for you, right?

"Yes, sir."

This nice policeman shifts his weight before he began again, more carefully. "Now, he can't hear you over there, so you can be honest with me. Did you want to come here and be with this boy? Because if you didn't I could take care of the situation."

"No, officer. I came here on my own."

You dirty whore.

After Nice Boy was allowed back in the car, the officer leaned in one more time.

"I don't want y'all around here. This place isn't safe, okay? We've been finding some dead bodies out here lately, so it's a dangerous area. If y'all want to be together for that stuff, go to his house or her house or go get a hotel room—I don't care where y'all go, but it's not safe to do it on a deserted street. Okay?"

"Yes, sir."

"You kids be safe, now."

And he left.

As we sat in silence, I thought about how there probably weren't any dead bodies, but he just wanted to scare us into being responsible. It could have been dangerous, though; there was always a possibility that someone would drive up and down deserted roads looking for lovers to hack to pieces. If we had been kidnapped, nobody would have known we were gone for some time. I thought about how lucky I was to be with someone who cared about me, who loved me and just wanted to spend an evening under the stars. How special our night was, even more special now that we had this memory, this close call with both serial killers and the law.

Nice Boy looked at me, his eyes wide. "Tell him I'm sleeping?"

"May I remind you that you put your seatbelt on your topless body? And I told him I was eighteen."

"You could have gotten in so much trouble for that!"

"I know! I panicked! I did it for you!"

"Oh, there he is again. Driving by."

"Thank you, Officer Friendly!"

"Kids, I mean it, you need to drive away from here."

"You got it."

[This letter was defaced by boys in class. Their notes are in bold.]

9, April, 1991

Once I look it's over. I know it. I won't look this time, that's all. Just keep my eyes closed and my head turned and I won't have to worry. I won't feel the pain, the anguish, the sorrow. I won't feel the agony, the anticipation, the expectation. I will not look and then I'll be okay. Oh, still my mind wanders. How it wanders and conjures up images of solitude and despair. My strength is crumbling. My mind is getting carried away. Unwanted images fill my head and manipulate my emotions. My hormones run wild. My hands scream to feel you. My arms yearn to hold you. My mind is chanting your name. **[Matt]** My lips long for yours. **[Matt oh Matt]** My eyes are searching for yours. **[My stomach is yearning for a sandwich. A Matt sandwich yum mmmm]** My head turns to face you. I take a deep breath, I open my eyes…I see you. I looked. It's over. **[I wish you were wearing a mask. Pants would be nice, too. You really suck.]**

Part Two

Getting Serious About Sex

I Turned Sixteen and Got Really Horny on April 15th...

...for when you are sixteen, there is no Tax Day.

15, April, 1991

Moving at speeds faster than I could ever imagine our bodies are like one. My eyes are slammed tight, my fists are clenched, my toes are curled.

So, I'm sixteen. I have a boyfriend, the one who used to be with K. Since I'm making out with a boy who has no problem declaring himself awake the entire time, I'm more than a little excited about it. Therefore I can't just write him a *note*. Notes are for friends! He's my *boyfriend*!

He was also a very grown-up kind of boyfriend. He had his own money, which he would use to create a music studio in the spare room of his house, or install black and white tile in his room, or buy a lot of bondage-type leather clothes.

That sounds like I was dating a future DJ King of Gayland, but I'll just let you know that because of Facebook I know that he is married to a lady and has a child. Alternative/Goth in the nineties was a sexually ambiguous time for fashion. There was my boyfriend in all that tight leather, there I was dressed like Eddie Vedder. We weren't getting nominated into the Homecoming Court, is all I'm saying.

Anyway, he had a very grown-up kind of life, which meant we were allowed to be in his room with the door shut, so I reached a new base. Like, pretty close to third. I had new wants and desires and confusions and words! I had new words and I was itching to use them.

15, April, 1991

Now. Now. Why aren't you here right now? I need you. I have to see you. I have to touch you. I have to run my fingers along the inside of your legs. Now. I need to feel the pounding, the pulsing, the pressure. I have to have you near me. I have to have you on me. I have to have you in me…if only your voice swirling in my head.

Don't get too close! Just close enough for voice-swirls, please. And can I just check your shoelaces for their color? I know that's weird, but I've had some experiences in the past that make me constantly check now. And have you ever had a sleeping disorder? No? Great. Then please let me continue to run my fingers along the inside of your legs.

Now. I need to have you touch me. I need your tongue to dance along my body and—

I abruptly stop myself and restart, but please note that each time I take a moment to record the date.

15, April 1991

You say my name.

[*explodes in orgasm*]

Never before had my name been filled with such sexual energy. Never before had my name been laced with lust. Never before had the sound of my name made my toes curl.

There will be a lot of toes curling in upcoming letters. My toes curl so tightly sometimes you'll swear Dorothy's house has just dropped on top of me.

I feel you near me. I feel your hands approaching mine. I cannot see you—for it is pitch black. I know not where I am or how I got there. It does not matter. I am beside you, and my world is now complete.

I can feel your breath on my skin. I feel you get closer. Your lips reach mine for a touch, a pause, and you retract. My lips beg for more. I rise to the tips of my toes to have my pleasure again. You reward me with another kiss as your hands grasp the sides of my shirt and hold on tight. A fierce and rapid jerk from your arms encloses my body in yours. I can feel your heartbeat against my ear, and the feel of your shirt is against my cheek. My body begins to crave for your flesh. I take off your shirt and kiss your chest, feeling your breathing becoming more rapid by your heaving chest under my mouth. My fingertips skid up your back, and rest on the backs of your shoulders.

Does he have a heaving chest, or am I the dude in this awkward erotica? Oh, yes. I've created my own genre: *awkwardica.*

April 15, 1991

It starts from my neck. The heat from your mouth engulfs my body as your tongue dances on my skin. Your hands hold me with strength and experience, strategically placed in places that drive me wild. I have to close my eyes for fear of fainting from pleasure. You move downward slowly, inch by inch, tracing my sweat with your tongue.

I am getting braver. I bet this means I delivered this letter. And I'm remembering right now that these awkwardicas were collected by this boyfriend and he saved them in a box on his living room shelf, so either one day his mother found them or (hopefully) he set them all on fire sometime before Prom.

The speed increases. But slowly, every nerve is alive and tingling and fully aware of every action, every sensation. My hands slide from your shoulders down to your back, my fingers kneading your muscles to the rhythm of the circles that your mouth is making on my stomach.

That's a complicated move!

You go lower still.

Fists clenched, toes curled, eyes shut tight, muscles pulled in, I feel like I am about to explode or faint. I will either die or live forever. Your pace is steady, and your fingers are tracing small patterns on my thigh. My mind is chaos, a land of confusion.

I do wish this letter came with an interpretive dance.

My strength is crumbling. You look at me. Whisper: "I love you."

I go wild.

No such thing as morals or manners. Fuck cautiousness. Fuck self-consciousness. Fuck it all. Just take me. Grind. Pound.

Have I mentioned before that I listened to a lot of Nine Inch Nails?

Twist. Moan. Pulse. Push. Make me feel alive. Make me feel unreal. Tease me. Taste me. Tantalize me. Hold me. Hurt me. Love me. Fuck me. Do it now. Touch me. Teach me. Taunt me. Make me live. Make me learn. Make me sweat. Make me exhausted but give me the stamina to go on. Feel me. Let me feel you. Let me slink my hands down your body and back up again only to retrace my journey once more. Take me up—higher and higher—faster and faster—harder and harder—until I've hit the ultimate, the ecstacy [*sic*], the bliss. Then bring me down. Gently. Slowly. Every sensation slowly fades away as I open my eyes and my breathing slows and I fall dead in your arms knowing that I will always love you.

One night, if you're nice enough to me, like if you take me out and we get drunk enough that I trust you as if we're fifteen, I will perform this letter for you. There are no awards for spoken awkwardica—YET. But I'm telling you I perform this with EGOT-level passion. (Buy the audiobook!)

...For this does not give justice to the last two days...

She turns off the lights and looks out the window. The city lights play on her face, her eyes reflect a blinding glare. She begins to sway to the music. She knows not the words; she does not mind. She closes her eyes and dances alone. Twirling and whirling—her only partner is the light shining up at her through tinted windows. Her audience consists of shadows.

One moves.

A scuffle, a shuffle, a shift. She opens her eyes and looks down. She cannot see, but she knows it is him. He places his hand on her ankle. He rises to his knees and slides his hand higher, higher, until it rests on her thigh— momentarily. His hand slides up her dress to the flesh of her stomach and back down again. He stands, hands still on her thighs, and kisses her

Lightly

On her neck. She is whole.

They move in unison to the music, and his hands continue to move

Slowly

Over her body. She loses the strength to stand, for her body becomes a quivering mass of desires. They sink to the floor, he lays beside her.

He starts at her toes.

Her back arches at his caresses. Her breathing becomes faster, his touches become softer...slower.

She bites her lip.

His tongue dances along her leg, he kisses her knee.

Her toes curl.

His hands slowly grope her skin higher and higher, resting at her hips. He kisses her stomach.

She sighs. And curls her legs under. She begins to grind— by some uncontrollable reflex—an animal instinct that only he has the power to tap into.

But he knows exactly how to play her.

He rises, kisses her breasts, and skids his tongue up her neck to her chin.

Kisses again.

And slides to her ear. Her breathing is quicker now— more gasps, and she moans under her breath.

He smiles.

And unclothes her.

His touches electrify her senses. She bites hard on her lip to silence her ecstacy [sic]. She grasps his shoulder as their bodies move in syncopated time.

She begins to move faster.

He keeps his pace, which spins her more into a frenzy, her desires overwhelm her; For she has never felt like this before.

So alive.

One of his hands rests on her leg. It is the most sexually arousing feeling she has ever experienced. Every cell in her body craves him. The scent of him. The smell of him. The feel of him.

She moves faster.

He keeps with her pace. She bites down on her lip harder and sets her jaw in determination. She can feel everything. She is aware of his breath on her neck, his toes on her legs, his wrist moving between her thighs.

She is closer.

Closer. Faster. Faster. Her breathing is quicker, lighter.

She tenses.

Every emotion in her is reeling. Every muscle dances in pleasure. Her body spasms in ecstacy [sic].

Her love for him fuels the fire, and she craves him to the core of her body.

She is one.

Her muscles relax, and she encloses him in her arms for a kiss.

I love you, he says.

So she felt.

Going Down, But Not Necessarily Understanding the Mechanics of Such a Term

I found this letter in my folder twice. *Handwritten* twice. One of them has a rip, which I taped together. This means I liked this enough to save *two* first drafts and deliver a third—or it's possible (but not probable) (but I hope so) (but I'm sure that's not what happened) that I never delivered this second draft. What could possibly keep me from sharing this masterpiece?

16, April, 1991

"Excuse me," you say, as you bump my shoulder when you enter.

"First floor?" I ask, feeling the blush on my face at the embarrassment of my voice changing at the sight of your beauty. You nod, lean back, your head touching the back of the small room that only our two bodies encompass.

I think maybe we've found the reason. At least, I hope somewhere I was like, *Hmm. Am I really ready to send someone super-soft-core elevator porn? Is this relationship strong enough for fluffy-core porn? Is any?*

The elevator plummets, and as my insides rise with the fall, my head spins as well.

I have vertigo for you. Now let's do it—quickly, because this building only has three floors. How long does sex take? I truly have no idea.

I can't stop staring at you. Your eyes are fixed on mine as well.

"Hello," you say.

I open my mouth. I pause. What do I say? I love you. I lust you. I want you. Nothing seems logical.

And yet, all things I've actually said to real, live people by this point in my life, all within the first twenty-four hours of meeting them.

"I..."

The lights go out.

The elevator stops.

You step closer to me. I step closer to you.

I feel your hand on my thigh.

A moan escapes my lips. You silence it with a kiss. A long, hard, pounding, probing kiss. Your hands keep working, they've slid up my dress and grasp to rip off my underwear. You pause. I feel you smile. You know I'm not wearing any.

I think I was reading a lot of Anaïs Nin and I'd gotten it into my head that fooling around in public places was a lot of fun. I had that thought because I couldn't fool around in any private places, so I suppose I was taking what I could get and romanticizing it. I mean, if you can call this romanticizing.

This makes you more aggressive, and you pull my dress off of me. My hands are working as well, tearing at your shirt, peeling off your pants, touching your skin gently. Your breathing is rapid, my tongue is in your ear. Your hands are sliding up and down, my back begins to arch as I push myself toward you and you push yourself in.

When two bodies are in this position I'm not sure that it's physically possible for a penis to enter a vagina.

Everything is in sync—right down to our heartbeats. We move as if we've known each other forever.

I cannot think of a less sexy thought. *Let's have sex like we've known each other forever: "I can't remember, am I the one who likes anal, or is it you? Just do it, it doesn't matter. Hurry up; we're missing Mad Men."*

Your fingers tease parts of my body as my tongue teases parts of yours. We move fast—faster, your hands are gripping my sides as you hold me against the wall with a dominating force. My body is tingling, but unbelievably aware.

"So, I thought I'd come in for a check-up, doctor."

My eyes are closed as you kiss my face and the elevator starts again. We are moving faster as the elevator drops. Falling faster. Moving faster. Our screams unite in pitch. We hold—muscles tightened, nerves on fire, head spinning, heart screaming, backs arched to the fullest degree, and we both feel the rush. The elevator continues to soar downward and our moans begin to fade as we open our eyes and the elevator smashes to the ground with a shattering impact that takes us both into a world beyond.

Smoosh! Death sex! Has TV taught you nothing? That's what happens when you're fucking a stranger when you're a teenager—death or pregnancy!

This is not the last of my awkardica, but I do go back to my roots for a second. I don't want this boy to think I only want him for his hands and fingers.

June 18, 1991

ACTUAL BOY'S NAME—

I feel horrible.

I am the happiest that I have ever been. I am the most peaceful that I have ever been. I am the most alive that I have ever been.

But yet, I feel horrible.

This is probably a letter not to that boy but to hormones. Please remember that this is the first time I've been in a relationship that wasn't either completely imaginary or entirely fueled by my constant affection. I believe this was the first boy to tell me that he loved me and wasn't just testing out the phrase or trying to get laid.

All of these feelings are because of you. Because of the way you make me feel when you talk to me, when you touch me, even when you look at me. My inner peace is because of the way you hold me, shelter me, love me.

It is crazy to me to realize that we could have been legally married if our parents gave consent. This is what he wanted to do at sixteen. And why laws are important.

Boys wanting to marry me before we ever got to college became a constant in my future relationships. It will be one of the reasons things don't work out with the boy I'm dating in this letter. It will be part of what eventually ends things later with Nice Boy. It will even cause problems with my first college boyfriend, who will assume I'd want to drop out of school to have children. My parents would tell you this happens because I had an unhealthy fixation on whomever I was dating that cultivated a co-dependency that made young boys feel so overprotective they began to treat me like property. I would tell you it was because THEY LOVED ME SHUT UP YOU DON'T EVEN KNOW HIM WHY ARE YOU IN MY ROOM CAN WE HAVE CHICKEN FOR DINNER???

> You tell me your dreams of the two of us lost in paradise. You tell me your fears of being without me. You tell me how you are obsessed with my beauty.

I am flattered.

And misquoting, I'm betting.

> Still, I feel horrible because I lack the guts to tell you how I feel about you. I don't know why. I don't know where it comes from—my parents, past relationships, or maybe it's just me. But I want to tell you how I feel about you because you mean the entire world to me and to keep something from you as important as how I feel about you is wrong.

I think I'd started reading different books. This has to be it. Or I saw *Dangerous Liaisons*. My tone has completely changed from when I was fifteen and pining. It's as if as soon as the same boy made out with me more than once, I decided I'd become a "woman," and it was time to deal with my life as a real woman would. With maturity, grace, and an admission that perhaps it is her own fault that she's struggling with her inability to discuss her emotions...which, come on, clearly, I've got no problem discussing my emotions.

> I feel horrible because every time that I look at you I want to tell you how much I need you, crave you, love you—but every time I open my mouth to do it, I instead close it with a kiss on your neck, your chest, your face.

I might be scared to say something because I've learned that telling a boy you like him is the fastest way to make him not like you. It is a lesson I immediately forget every single time I learn it. I will go on to learn this lesson countless times. I will be teased about my inability to learn this lesson as recently as last week.

> I hate not telling you my feelings, and I'm beginning to think that this letter is just another cheap easy way out. But I think that just saying
>
> I love you
>
> doesn't mean anything.

Yes, I wrote it out like that on paper. I put that "I love you" on its own line for dramatic effect. It's three very important words, you guys. You can't just put them in the mix with other words. How will he know what I'm trying to say? This confession needs its own line, just to be clear, just in case this boy doesn't get the complexities of what I'm throwing down.

> Three words that are supposed to sum up all of these feelings inside of me? How? It can't.
>
> I love you
>
> doesn't tell you that you are constantly on my mind. It doesn't let you see my dreams that—

Oh, boy. Buckle up.

> —you are always in. It doesn't let you taste the tears that I shed when I can't be close to you.
>
> I love you
>
> is an abstract phrase. My emotion for you is not abstract.

Well. Technically—

I can see it in the way my eyes watch your body longingly, lingering on places I'd long to touch. I can hear it in the way I say your name—much like some people say

God.

We are on page three. It only gets worse from here.

I can smell it when you are near and when the smell of your hair or your clothes drives me wild. I can taste it on your flesh. And I can feel it.

I can feel it.

Through every part of my body. Every part of me is infactuated [*sic*] with you. I have you captured in my mind.

That spelling mistake kills me, because obviously I thought it meant being so enamored with a person that you memorize every fact. It's the smart person's love affair. *I'm infactuated with you. Go ahead. Test me. I'm ready for the finals week of your heart.*
The next TWO FULL PAGES of this letter is a list of things that I have captured of him in my mind.

The way you hold me.
The way you smile.
The way you kiss.
The feel of your heartbeat against my chest.
The sound of your whisper.
The way you put your arm around me.
The way you skate.
The way you make music.
The way your hair falls over your eyes.
The way you push it out of the way.
The way your chin dimples.
The way your mind works.
The sound of your voice saying "I love you."

The way you walk.
The way you laugh.
The way your breath feels on my ear.
The way your hands move.
The sound of your voice.
The feel of your body.
The way you make me laugh.
The way you challenge my mind.
The way you hold my hand.
The way you kiss my forehead.
The way you cry.
The way you sleep.
The way you eat.

It was really nice of this boy to date me for as long as he did. I don't think that, until this very moment, I ever gave him enough credit for hanging in there with me.

These things I keep within my heart, along with everything else about you that is all supposed to sum up to that little phrase

I love you.

The other day I was sitting on my bed thinking about you. Nothing in particular, just thinking about you and how you've changed my life—

I'm jealous that Little Pam had this kind of disposable time.

—when I looked up into the mirror and saw this huge smile on my face. I don't remember smiling, it was just there, like a reflex to your name.

I can't seem to get you out of my mind. This morning I was wondering if I went down the alphabet, would there be any letter in the alphabet that wouldn't remind me of you? I went down the list, and I only couldn't figure out one for Z.

At least I knew no boy wanted to learn I'd spent my morning trying to find out if I had enough good thoughts about our relationship to fill an alphabet. I bet that's why I have this letter. I probably rewrote it without this part and gave him the rest...including that list which is so embarrassingly not in alphabetical order!

(P.S. There is totally a list. I found it. No, I will not share it with you. There. We have found my one limit. Alphabetical lists.)

I wish there was a way to show love—

There's a virgin waving a flag of surrender if I've ever seen one. *"Gee, if only there was a way to SHOW love. Do you have any ideas? Because it's not ladylike for me to suggest we take off our clothes and do it all the way."*

—because I am not good at this talking stuff. I know how I feel, but somehow I can't even write it because it is so complex. It is so unreal.

I mean, is love more about the sound of someone's whisper, or the way they skate?

I've never experienced love like this before. If I seem unsure, it is because everything is so new to me.

And by that I mean the fact that you seem to like me back is really very new to me.

All of these feelings sometimes scare me.

And by that I mean I am scared you are going to break up with me at any moment. Like now. Or now. Or now. And now I'm scared that since you haven't broken up with me yet, it means you want to break up with me, but you don't know how to tell me because you're so nice and you will be my boyfriend who secretly doesn't want to be my boyfriend and that would be the WORST THING IN THE WORLD so you might as well break up with me now before you realize you want to break up with me, oh God sixteen is the worst.

> Not enough to run, I'd never do that. I'm sorry, [BOY], but you are stuck with me.

GOT IT? STUCK. WITH ME.

> You can't leave me because

> I love you

> and I'll follow you everywhere.

GOT IT? EVERYWHERE. FOLLOW YOU. YOU CAN'T LEAVE ME. PLEASE DON'T LEAVE ME. Where are you going? What's wrong? Did we just break up? Why?

> I need you. My life is nothing without you.

…for about two more months and then summer will be over and I'll end up in theatre arts and then my life will be, like, theatre, school, rehearsal, homework, and then you. Hope you understand. But until then: you are my entire life and I will suck every available second of yours into mine because THAT IS THE ONLY WAY I UNDERSTAND LOVE.

> I wish I could say these things to you without being nervous, but that is something I will have to learn to do. I *love you*. For lack of a better phrase I will keep repeating that. *I love you*.

> Forever.

And then it just ends there because apparently I threw my journal aside and ran around the empty house screaming SIXTEEN IS SO CLOSE TO BEING AN ADULT—WHY WON'T MY PARENTS JUST LET ME MOVE OUT AND LIVE MY LIFE? GAH!

Is this the third letter wherein I confess to a boy that I love him but the whole time I try to make it seem like I'm talking about something else and/or someone else entirely? That is super depressing.

I got grounded, I'm guessing, from this next letter, which wasn't in a journal but instead scrawled on this huge piece of art paper, like I was going to soak it in tea and burn the edges and then scroll it up to carrier pigeon it over to my beloved, confined as such was I to a parental prison.

July 22, 1991

> Where are you? I call for you. I yell for you. I scream for you. Yet I cannot find you.

Or maybe he hasn't returned my call in the past fifteen minutes.

> I need you—don't you see that? You are all that I have. You are all that I want.

He's probably just in the bathroom and I've gone into a panic.

> You are all that I am. Yet I cannot have you. Trapped in this prison away from you makes me feel as if I've been sent to live without my heart.

Okay, no, I was right the first time. So grounded. I'm not going to interrupt this next paragraph, but please imagine it's being read by Will Ferrell wearing a monocle.

> Sent to deteriorate without the one thing keeping me going and forcing me to live. I love you. Can't you see that? You leave me—I know you don't realize it, or mean to, but you do. You leave me here alone in a hell. Nothing keeps me happy. Nothing keeps me content. Nothing feels right. Television bores me, books seem futile (for my tears blur my vision anyway), and music loses all of its power and beauty.

Keep the monocle on Will Ferrell, but now through the next part imagine he's slowly taking off his pants.

> Don't you realize all that you mean to me? I can't survive without you. I can't think without you. I can't even breathe without you. Your voice is my energy. Your face is my heartbeat. I need you.

So now imagine monocled, pantsless Will Ferrell standing in a spotlight, center stage, using the following as his audition for the tenth grade theatre arts production of *Go Ask Alice*.

> Every once in a while I can hear your voice right behind me. I swear that I can hear you say my name. I whirl around—eager to run to you—but there is nothing, no one. For it is my own mind, my own head playing tricks on me, teasing me, taunting me. For what reason I cannot figure out. All I know is that this yearning for you is so real, so powerful, that my mind is willing to re-create an imaginary you just to keep the rest of me happy. It doesn't work, obviously.

The letter abruptly ends there because someone probably walked unannounced into my room.

I'm clearly still struggling with how to feel about all the feelings I'm feeling in my feeling parts. I try it out with some poetry that stinks worse than a Renaissance Faire.

SANDLEWOOD DREAMS [sic]

> The scent of Sandlewood incense [*sic*] Mingled with the burn of sweat
> Linger and swirl in my room.

This one is better if you read it like you're Julianne Moore desperately trying to make sense of this speech she has to give in front of the President, as she's grabbed the wrong piece of paper and instead of an impassioned plea for gun control or women's rights, she's stuck reciting the following:

> A thousand dreams fall like snowflakes, dripping
> From the ceiling that I stare at.
> They dance around my head.
> Anxious to land
> And fill my mind.
> Melting the feel of you
> On my skin.
> The smell of you
> In my head.
> I ache for you.
> A yearning deep within
> Calls your name in desparate [*sic*] chants.
> I give to you
> My mind and soul.
> The deepest part of me.
> I call for you
> Yet no one answers
> But the lonely rain drumming a sad song
> On my unclothed windowpane.
> I can see you.
> My eyes create your outline
> Shadowed in my doorway.
> (I can almost see your smile.)

The parentheses in all of my teen works show how much I thought I was very skilled at writing. (The parentheses in my present day works are all apologies.)

> I can hear you.
> Your laugh. Your voice. The sound of my name on your
> lips.
> I can feel you.
> Your kiss. Your touch. Your skin.
> I tremble.
> I open my mouth to call for you

And an image falls inside.

Again, it is a shame this book isn't illustrated. Can a fallen mouth image show up on dental exams? It's probably not covered under my insurance, anyway.

We are walking down a winding road
Barefoot. Linking arms.
We reach a brook.
You pick me up to carry me over the water
(such a gentleman)
But you slip and we fall—
Into a kiss.

Nice.

I open my eyes and I hear our laughter trail off in my
ears.
And my need for you has increased tenfold.
I need you more than just tonight.
Tomorrow night and beyond.
I love you.
It moves me to say.
And I tremble when I hear myself
Voicing my hidden emotion.
Sometimes I must shout out
The constant murmur in my ear
And let the world know
I am alive
I am in love
With you.

In the end, this relationship got complicated, because he was ready for me to move out of my house to marry him. My parents, unaware of this fact but somehow sensing this boy very much wanted to take their child away from them, continued to ground me with increasingly trumped-up charges and wildly inappropriate lengths of imprisonment. Summer ended and a mishap with my junior-year fall schedule resulted in my getting placed in my third-choice elective: Theatre Arts. I told my parents I had homework after school, but instead I went to an audition.

I got a part. And everything changed.

My grown-up relationship wasn't strong enough for my newly intense after-school schedule. He'd get frustrated when I couldn't spend hours with him locked away in his room. I'd get frustrated when he didn't support my passion for the arts. My parents, who normally said I didn't have time for extra-curriculars and should focus on my schoolwork, were suddenly overjoyed when I told them this alternative to doing homework at my boyfriend's house. Why, they practically *insisted* I push aside my calculus books to practice my monologues. If my parents were so happy for me, why wasn't he? When the fights got too big and he eventually asked me to choose—either him or acting—I did what any decent woman who loved with all of her heart would do.

I bought a Ben Nye make-up kit in Fair: Light-Medium and I never looked back.

First impressions are
Auditions for
Relationships.

Have you references?
Experience?
Prove your talents in a smile
A handshake, a hug.
Your scent is your resume.
Your laughter your monologue.
Rehearsals? We'll call you.
Next…

Because in the Dark,
You Are at Your Smallest.

November 1991

"I love you."

There. I said it. Now he'll have to talk to me. I can't believe I said it. He's not saying anything. Maybe he didn't hear me.

"I love you."

"I heard you."

Oh.

Okay, he heard me.

There is another reason that last relationship ended, and why every relationship of mine that existed in the real world, outside of my own head or journal, would end up having serious problems in the latter half of every year in that space between school starting and Thanksgiving break.

In an effort to breeze over the extremely personal and no fun to read: shitty things can happen to you when you're a kid, and that's because grown-ups can suck. One night, one hour, even one minute of this kind of shitty stuff changes you forever. Your childhood ends, and that's it. And one of the worst parts in an endless list of worst parts is how you aren't prepared; you aren't a part of it. It happens to you. It alters you. And then it lives inside of you and only you forever. Other parties involved go on with their lives, sometimes never having to even apologize for destroying an innocent person's sense of self.

It happened to me, and I lived with it for years believing it was firmly a part of my past, something tucked away and safely hidden where it could never touch me again.

But then I started kissing boys. We'd be alone in the dark and things would resurface. Things inside of me that were raw and angry, things I didn't understand. These shockingly scary emotions would shoot through me from something as innocuous as a boy trying to touch my ear in the dark. Suddenly I'm having panic attacks and disassociating and there's no way a thirteen-year-old girl knows how to turn to a thirteen-year-old boy and say, *"Please stop. I think I'm having some childhood trauma issues that are resurfacing now that I'm beginning to experience sexual situations."* And even if she does find a way to say that, probably with all those clinical terms because she's a dork, there's even less of a chance a thirteen-year-old boy can hear that without thinking, *This girl wants to break up.*

Year after year, for way too long, I'd get panic attacks in September. I tried talking to my parents, but I stumbled with the words and my father couldn't let himself hear the truth. I tried talking to teachers, but they never knew how to react. One night I called a hotline I found in the Yellow Pages. The number had been disconnected. I took it as a sign that I was supposed to deal with this all by myself.

I'd grab my lighter and I'd burn my wrist and I'd try to pull the inside pain outside, to look at it and deal with it, clean it with hydrogen peroxide and wrap it in bandages until it could scab and fall off. I wouldn't have even minded the scar, because then I could hold it up to the boy I loved and say, *"It's this part here, that's bothering me. Not you. I don't know how to handle it, so it makes me unable to handle you."*

I did stop sharing the truth with people because even though I felt like I was letting someone in on my huge secret, that I was showing them how much they mattered by getting to know the darkest, most terrified part of me, sometimes people would view it as a responsibility, or—worse—a burden. Once they got their arms filled with my damage, my baggage, they looked at me differently. Some treated me differently. I'm not just talking about the boys, here, and I'm not just talking about my youth. People didn't know how to handle it, so gradually I stopped talking about it. I stopped letting it be the ritual that inducted someone into my *real* life.

I wish I could say it was a decision based on strength and wisdom, or at least a great therapist, but the fact is I stopped telling everyone who would listen what happened to me and how it could become the monster in my relationships because certain people made me feel like I was the one with the problem. That it wasn't such a big deal, and I should be over it.

That always infuriated me. It still does. Nobody asks for this to happen to them, so they shouldn't be expected to just shut up about it so that other people stop feeling uncomfortable that it happened.

The young boys who ran away back then, I can hardly blame them. How could someone handle all of those love letters in his locker, combined with all of her feelings and then also handle knowing the secret to all of her fragility? How could one boy handle all of that and still study for a Trig exam?

I know it was just too much. I know it now. But back then I only had an idea that it was overwhelming. That I was overwhelming.

I stopped talking about it and instead kept trying to write it away. Write it away and it can be gone. Even now. Right here. I'm still trying to write it away. Every word I write, every story I tell will be another effort to put more space, more time, more words, more walls between me and that thing that wanted so hard to define me.

I no longer get scared in September. But I never put my guard all the way down. I keep my hands up and my fingers hovered over home row. Ready to fight.

Momento

12 Feb 1992

I sit among your memories. They are scattered at my feet and I can't help but wondering if I stand out. I wonder if even though I am clustered in with the tokens of your past, that I remain a part of your present, and will continue into the future. I am here merely to give parting words, but I wish they will remain forever in your ears—not as a memory but as a reminder. Of me. Do not forget me while you collect more tokens. Each momento [sic] tells a story, each trinket sings a song. Shine it, rub it, frame it…it speaks for itself as a triumphant or devastating moment in your life that you may or may not have chosen to remember. Regardless, it is burned into your mind as an image of you is burned into mine. I couldn't forget you if I tried. I'm sitting here among your things and I wonder if you notice me. You walk around me, stuffing some of the memories in your bag—those you want to keep with you forever. You close your bag and look around, I notice the tear that runs down your beautiful face. I stand to touch you…to kiss it away or maybe just to brush up against your hand. You lift your head and your eyes meet mine. You walk over, take me into your warm arms and kiss me. You let go. You grab your bag of trinkets and walk out the door. I begin to run after you but I trip over one of your old shoes and I fall to the floor and remain there crying. Goodbye.

Me: Oh, this is embarrassing. This is a story I wrote about a boy moving away.

Mom: (Looking over my shoulder) No! This is the other story I was asking you about. If you had it.

Me: What other story?

Mom: This is the one you wrote about the cat.

Me: …What?

Mom: This story. You wrote it as the cat. It was a letter from Nutso. To you.

Me: …No.

Mom: Yes! You turned it in. At school.

Me: NO.

Mom: What's wrong? I think it's clever. It's the cat! But you can't tell it's the cat.

Me: No, you cannot.

Mom: But now when you read it, when you know it's the cat? You can tell.

Me: Oh, God.

Mom: Stop being so dramatic. I think it's clever. My baby's a writer.

It Gets Marginally Better

This is the story of the boy who only got this one letter, but the story of him was a defining moment, a milestone all too familiar to a girl like me.

14 Feb

A smile when the world is crumbling;

A laugh breaking through my tears.

Looking up when everything is tumbling;

Being brave through all my fears.

He was everything that could possibly be out of my league. He was older, more popular, better looking, wealthy, had his own car. He was also delightfully mysterious. He probably even drank alcohol and did drugs but didn't feel the need to brag about it.

And for some reason one seemingly random week, he noticed me.

It's possible I just made myself un-unnoticable. We were all in a play together, which meant school-enforced together time. I was pretty good at making myself visible when I wanted to be.

What really started my crush on him was when we had to do a scene together for UIL Duet Acting. For those of you who haven't gone through a Texas public high school curriculum (*Texas Forever!*), UIL competitions are interscholastic and statewide in everything from sports to music to academics. It's how you earn your letter jacket. For a couple of months I was a ringer for the debate team who needed a few desperate actors to round out their less dignified competitions.

Once I found out I could win a trophy for a monologue? That was *it*. I seized that challenge with more than the required intellect and passion, crafting a six-minute dramatic interpretation piece from the biography *Sybil*. I shamelessly parroted Sally Field until they had no choice but to hand me something shiny, if only to get me to crawl out from under the classroom's piano, where I was rabid and fetal, chanting, "*The people, and the people, and the people...*"

The boy who was out of my league, who I will call Soft Hair, for he had very soft hair that was long and could be pulled into a ponytail and that was just another thing about him that was different and wonderful, he and I were assigned a Duet Acting piece.

I remember he wanted to do something gritty and meaningful. He was pushing for a scene from *Bent*. I wanted a piece where we would have to pretend to slow-dance for five minutes before kissing goodbye and then I'd have a long, teary monologue about how he died of a heroin overdose after that and how I'll always love him.

I think you can guess which piece we ended up doing.

I wish that I could tell you what you mean to me. I open my mouth to tell you, and my voice cowers—hiding under the covers.

I don't know why my feelings aren't afraid of paper... perhaps because I don't have to look at you while I feel this way. I don't have to see your reaction, worry about how you're feeling, fear that you don't feel the same way.

That's not from the scene, but it might as well have been.

We did the teenaged-lover-dies-of-heroin scene and I think we got second place, I can't remember. But the important thing is by then I'd worn him down. I'd technically kissed him about twenty times in rehearsal and was hanging out with (near) him all the time once we were both in an upcoming play. Super Mario Brothers Boy was also cast in that show, so you can imagine how elated I was to be spending hours upon hours a day with the long-term unrequited love of my life and the most current unrequited love of my life. My poor little heart, it was ready to explode.

I'd get Soft Hair to drive me home after rehearsals as often as I could. Since Super Mario Brothers Boy and I were neighbors, Soft Hair would take us both home, usually dropping me off last. I know that seems like not any kind of sign at all, but when you are seventeen every inhale, every nostril flare, every errant scratch of an elbow or toe tap *means something about WHETHER OR NOT WE ARE GONNA GET TOGETHER.*

He would pull up outside my house, the car in idle, and he'd wait for me to leave.

I would not leave.

Instead, I would find excuses. So many excuses to stay. I'd ask about his car, the song we were listening to, his Birkenstocks, his hair. I'd ask about his hair, his skin, his eyes, and his hair. I'd compliment him on his performance that day. I'd gossip. I'd flirt. But he'd never turn off that ignition.

Until one day, when he did. And then he kissed me. Not for a rehearsal, not for practice, not just to get me to shut up. Maybe a little to get me to shut up. But he kissed me.

> Songs, flowers, candy, poems, sunsets…all are symbols of love, tokens of affection, the traditional trinkets of emotion. But this feeling, I think, is not tangible, it can't be represented by some inanimate object. I mean, what possible object on earth represents my total happiness?

Soft Hair wanted to hang out late on a Friday night. This was going to be tricky for many reasons, mostly because my parents hadn't met him and he was a grade older than I was. When they insisted he come over for dinner before I could go out, I tried to make it sound casual as I informed Soft Hair of the new rules.

"Oh, we could totally hang out tonight, but you just have to come by my house first and maybe eat or whatever."

"You don't want to do that," Super Mario Brothers Boy interrupted. "You don't want to have dinner with her parents. Trust me."

I tried to spin this obvious cockblock into something positive. "He's just jealous that they want to meet you."

"No, I'm not."

Soft Hair said, "Well. I'm not going to eat dinner at your parents' house unless [Super Mario Brothers Boy] comes with us."

SMB Boy shook his head. "No way. Her father hates me. We won't have a good time."

"Please!" I begged.

"Nope. But I'll hang out with you guys tonight."

I called my parents and informed them that I was unable to get either boy to come to dinner, but since they knew Super Mario Brothers Boy, they had no reason to worry about anything. Like I'm their harried assistant. "*So, sorry; they're not going to be able to make it to the meeting.*"

This was a very contentious time in my relationship with my parents, where a simple conversation about boundaries quickly escalated into screaming matches. This one was a doozy.

"You can't go out with someone we haven't met yet."

"But we don't have time to come home for dinner and go out."

"Then go out some other time."

I had to go out with Soft Hair Boy because if I didn't go out with him that night I wouldn't get to make out with him later. And Soft Hair would make out for a long time. No, specifically, Soft Hair would *kiss* for long periods of time. Kiss and hold hands and touch hair and kiss some more. I never knew it could be like that. There was no grinding or feeling-up or pushing for anything other than kissing and talking and kissing and talking and I couldn't believe he wanted to do all that kissing with me.

"Dad, no, that's not what they want to do! It's not a date. There are three of us. He's not even my boyfriend."

This wasn't technically true but maybe sort of was. I don't think I'd had the conversation with Soft Hair about whether or not we were officially dating, but I might have tested it by referring to him as my boyfriend just to see how he'd react. At that point it had been about a week and he'd had yet to correct me. Since he hadn't called himself my boyfriend out of his own mouth, I wasn't lying to my father.

Dad was sick of me at this point. "Fine. Then don't come home. We don't care. We are no longer your parents and we don't care what happens to you. Have a great life."

I know what he was going for there, and how he'd assumed I'd feel. I know he could only imagine after hearing something like that I'd say, *"Guys, I have to go home. I have disappointed my parents and I need to repair this relationship with some serious apologies because there's only so many days left before I'm off to college. So please, take me straight home, before another second passes without peace in my home life. My parents just want what's best for me, and it's time I let them know I appreciate how much they care."*

But I don't even think Dad was done slamming down the phone before I was doing a little dance.

"Great!" I said to the boys. "I'm free to go!"

I'm going out with Soft Hair on a date! On a date that also includes a boy I love with all my heart! I'm the luckiest girl in the woooorrrrlllld!

What can show how much I admire beauty, love, strength? Where can I go to show what I feel is the perfect example of hope, pride, beauty, strength and wisdom?

Once we were in his car, Soft Hair turned to us and asked, "So, can I just take you two anywhere I want to tonight? Can I show you things you've never seen? Can I show you what life can be like if you leave this town?"

COULD THIS NIGHT GET ANY BETTER?

Yes, Super Mario Brothers Boy and I said, nodding our heads off. *Yes, Soft Hair, yes! Take us to freedom! Show us how to live! Make us as cool as you! Does it come with being one year older, or is it because your parents are rich? What's it like to be so rich? Do you have more than one pair of jeans? That's so cool!*

He drove us straight to a part of downtown Houston that was dangerous and probably off-limits to three nerdy white kids from the suburbs.

"Where are we going?"

"A haunted insane asylum."

I just Googled it to make sure my memory wasn't exaggerating this moment, or if I'd somehow made up this part of the story entirely, but he must have taken us to Jefferson Davis Hospital, a one-time psych ward built on top of what was a cemetery used to bury Civil War soldiers. (Google tells me the building has since been renovated and is now artist lofts, so I guess you can visit it, for those of you making a map for a future Little Pam tour. (The saddest tour of all time.))

We pull up to the dark, abandoned, seriously-fucking-creepy building, and Soft Hair's getting out of the car because he's going to go exploring. There are two things I know I'm not brave enough to do: meet a ghost or break the law. Soft Hair wanted to do both of those things at once. Super Mario Brothers Boy, however, was down for the adventure. So, of course they leave, and of course I stay in the car and of course I realize THIS IS HOW THE GIRL GETS KILLED IN THOSE MOVIES and also I'm feeling stupid for not being brave because if I'd gone in there and gotten scared I could have at least held all the boys' hands right before I was killed, rather than my soon-dead fate where I'd end up only holding my own severed head.

After a million years, they came back unscathed, and Soft Hair announced the next place he needed to take us on his secret mental map. It was a coffee shop, music and art space called Downtown Grounds. I'd heard of it, but had never been allowed to go because it was downtown, which is where I was, which I could now do because I didn't have parents! Disowned forever! I was now a grown-up, living my grown-up life. So far it was going exactly how I'd always dreamed.

A coffee shop with cool people in it? Maybe they'd even ask me to do some spoken word poetry! I didn't have my journal, but I'm sure I could remember something I'd just written that brought to mind images of Shakespeare's Ophelia.

A picture worth a thousand words? Perhaps. The rose is still the rose is still the rose.

Or Gertrude Stein. The point is, I was so excited when we walked in, I was openly gawking. It was a warehouse building, and I remember a long walk before we reached a guy taking money and stamping hands. Soft Hair was friends with him and said he wanted to introduce us. The stamp guy was thin, with deep, pock-marked skin and bushy eyebrows. He wore a leather jacket because he was a hand-stamp guy taking money in front of a music venue.

Super Mario Brothers Boy asked for directions to the bathroom and headed off. I stood there taking it all in, planning my new parent-free life as a coffee shop girl who hung out with her journal and wrote while art was created all around her. Maybe I'd weave myself a hair wrap with some bells and beads. (I did do that, but not for another year or so.) (Shut up.)

Love? It isn't in the stars or inside the petals of the perfect flower. Love is merely but a state of mind.

Hand Stamp Guy asks Soft Hair why he wanted us to meet him.

"Because you're a stop on our special city tour," Soft Hair said. "I don't think [Super Mario Brothers Boy] has ever met a real gay man before."

"Oh. Well, then should we give him something interesting to remember me by?"

Maybe by now in the story you see what's coming. But listen, I really didn't. And it all kind of happened at once. Super Mario Brothers Boy returned from the bathroom and Soft Hair smiled at him before placing a hand on Hand Stamp Guy's shoulder, and then he leans down and then they're kissing and kissing and kissing and I'm backing up and I'm running and I'm running and I'm running—

—and I would have run all the way back to that insane asylum if I had to, but instead I just stood in the parking lot by the car and waited with all of the drama. I had all of the drama and none of the words for it. *Yet.*

SMB Boy was beside me, having followed me out. "Are you okay?" he asked.

Arms crossed, eyes wide, I turned my chin so fast and hard I could've cut somebody with my face. "*I. Don't. Know.*"

Poets and philosophers have been searching for an answer to this unexplainable emotion from within, caused by the aura of another. To me, the only thing that can explain why or how deep my emotions run is you. Just you. You don't have to say a word, only smile. The rest is self-explanatory.

Soft Hair climbed into his car and unlocked our doors. Once all three of us were back in our seats, in the dark, we sat in silence for a while.

I thought about how hard and confusing it must be to be a boy in high school in a small Texas town, how maybe he was trying to show us something bigger than we could understand just tonight. Maybe he had been inviting me and Super Mario Brothers Boy to join him in this semi-adult world where he's accepted for who he is and he never has to lie or pretend to be someone else. Maybe he was wondering if we felt like outsiders, too, and if we were sometimes confused about who we were and whom we loved.

Then I thought about all of our kissing, how it always stayed firmly on first base. Even if I'd let a hand slide up his thigh he'd find a way to gently push it away. He never tried to put his hand up my shirt, and if I "allowed" him to touch me by placing his hands directly on my chest, he'd quickly find a way up to my hair, which he'd smell or rest his cheek against while asking me various personal questions about Super Mario Brothers Boy.

It never occurred to me how odd it was that we both spent hours in that car talking about how great Super Mario Brothers Boy was. How cute he was. What clothes he wore. And if he liked us.

As I said before, there was no such thing as "gay" at that school. I didn't have any friends who identified themselves that way. It wasn't an option. By taking us on this tour of his city, Soft Hair was letting us see the most fragile part of him, his most hidden secret. He had to have been hoping we would take his hand and say, "*This is all okay.*"

It had been quiet for a while. I knew it was my turn to speak. So I took a deep breath and I asked the one question that made sense at that moment. I asked it from the bottom of my heart and at the top of my shaky lungs. My words pierced the heavy silence.

"Does this mean you want to break up?"

If you asked Super Mario Brothers Boy to list some of his favorite moments from our time together, this one would definitely be in the top three. But I couldn't understand any other reason he would want me to see him kiss another boy.

"No, it doesn't mean I want to break up," Soft Hair said, not without a hint of disappointment in his voice.

"Are you *sure*?"

"Yes."

"Because you'd tell me if you weren't sure, right?"

"I would."

"How do you know when you want to kiss boys and when you want to kiss girls?"

"I just do. Right now I only want to kiss you."

"Could you maybe not kiss boys the rest of the time we're together? Because it hurts my feelings."

"Do y'all want to go get some pancakes?"

We did.

Soft Hair held my hand as he drove us for late-night pancakes, the best food in the world when you are seventeen.

Three days later he broke up with me. That year he took a girl with a reputation for giving blow jobs to Prom. Her name was Kippy. And that's called Texas.

> There isn't a person alive who could debate the legitamacy [*sic*] of falling for someone when that someone stands before them to be judged, and that someone is you.

It's sometimes hard being that non-threatening, funny girl whom gay boys test their gayness upon. I know I'm not the only one, but at the time I had no idea there were others. It's a secret club where each member thinks she is the sole member. If there's an unspoken benefit to boys and girls feeling comfortable enough to come out sooner in their lives, it's all the heartache we'll save from the safe girls and nice boys who have no idea they are being chosen as the cover story, the temporary fix, or the final test.

I know it's long past the appropriate time to make one of these things, but I so wanted to make a video like:

"He was my best friend."

"He was funny, he was smart, and he loved hanging out with me."

"He helped me do my hair for Prom and got me super drunk."

"...and then he came out."

"...it turns out he was gay."

"...and then he told me he was gay."

"I saw him again after college...when I met his boyfriend."

"And it all made sense, but also: it hurt."

"It was a little painful, yes."

"I have never loved a man the way I loved him. I never will. He was everything I wanted."

"You learn to find someone else, but it's just not the same."

"It can't be the same. It's different. It gets different."

"It gets marginally better."

"It gets...tolerable."

"It gets mostly okay."

March 1, 1992

I tug the ends of his shirt from his pants and slide my hands lightly over the flesh of his back. My fingers dance on his newly formed goosebumps. He pushes himself up, his legs stradling [sic] mine, and pulls his shirt off over his head

with one arm.

The moonlight coming through the window bathes his skin in a blue glow. The shadows of his face hide not his beauty, and nature creates an overwhelming aura of sex around him.

I feel warm.

He slowly lowers on top of me again and kisses my lips.

Time is Not Equal (When Time = Mutual Masturbation)

I think this is a poem I wrote about making out that ends with someone masturbating on me? And maybe we're in a closet or something? And maybe it's the day I learned that penises don't stay hard after they ejaculate?

March 23, 1992

*...Some Day I Will Be Able
to Write a Decent Poem...*

Two forms in the night—
Wanting only to please each other.
Harmless lies brought them there;
Conniving made them one.
They are finally alone.

That's some flowery talk for "sneaking out." Also, I'm in love with the title I gave this poem, where I clearly thought I'd written something way better than "decent," but felt it best to maintain an air of modesty.

They caress;
Kiss.
Enclose each other with love,
For it is equal.
But time is not.

I have no idea what that means, but the important thing is it sounds like I have a lot of knowledge about what things mean.

> They begin in unison,
> But his emotions become too strong—
> Overwhelming.
> She tells him to concentrate on himself.
> He does.

I have a very real hindsight fear that I once gave a boy a poem I'd written about his premature ejaculation. I'm sure this is all fictional, I say to anybody reading this who may have once done third base on my leg. Do not worry, I bet this isn't about you. (It might be. Sorry.)

> He feels incredible.
> Invincible.
> Power.
> Love.
> For her.

"He feels. He will have to change. His underpants."

> But alas—
> Time is not on their side.
> She yearns to feel him too;
> To feel the power.
> But she cannot.

"No, I guess it's not going to happen. I guess because you're trying to get me off in this parking lot and I'm too worried that people can see us."

> They break apart
> In silence.
> She feels a void.
> He feels selfish.
> Both are foolish.

He loves her.
He wants her to be happy.
He needs her.
He loves the way she feels.
Love is power alone.

She loves him.
She wants him to be happy.
She needs him.
She loves the way he feels.
Love is power alone.

He kisses her.
They unite again.

It seems like it was maybe a rough day for me, but I tried to spin it with my irrepressible romanticism disguised as a pep talk. Don't worry, Little Pam. There will be other boners.

Part Three

Getting Serious About Issues

Our Teenage Muse

I read *The Bell Jar* and got really into Sylvia Plath. I suppose it's just what teen girls do, but there was something about Sylvia's transition from magazine intern to suicide poet that I found extremely aspirational. I chose Sylvia Plath as the subject of my research paper that semester for English class, and I do believe I cited myself as a source when I quoted the following, which I included at the back of my report:

March 5, 1992

One looks to darkness for the light.
One hopes for daylight to find the night.
A cycle—never ending.
A circle—never bending.
It's repetition proves it's never right. [sic] [sic] [sic] [sic]

I also included the following masterpiece. All the backstory you need is that I'd never once done a single drug. Not one puff or pill. I'd never had a drink, I'd never smoked a cigarette. Never dropped a tab or lit a spoon on fire or cracked a whippet. (Is that how you spell it?) A couple of years later at a college freshman party, I will see someone smoking from a water bong and freak the fuck out that there were crackheads in the room. That's how little I knew about drugs and what it felt like to take them. That didn't stop me from assuming I knew enough to write this:

FOR SYLVIA

I close my eyes and wait. They begin to hit in five-minute intervals. Each one doubling in intensity.

I guess I believed that if you swallowed a bunch of pills you felt them one at a time as they "hit" your system.

The first brings a strange hum in my ear. It builds stronger and stronger, louder and louder.

Perhaps I had swallowed a bee, with my ear.

I bring my hands to my ears as the second hits. A tremble strikes my hands and I can no longer keep them over my ears, not even able to make them clasp each other. I pop my knuckles one by one, joint by joint, hoping to release some of the tension.

Wait, I've lost the muscle coordination to simply cup my hands to my ears, but now I'm able to crack each knuckle?

Each crack of my knuckle is multiplied in sound a million fold. It hurts to hear.

That hurts to read.

I shiver with cold. I pull the blanket around my body, the frayed edges brush against my nose and my skin screams from the friction. I'm afraid to open my eyes. The third hits, and brings with it a multitude of colors, reds and greens swirl before my eyes.

Sounds like this all would've been more fun if I'd started with the third pill.

I hear voices. Singing mournful woes. Death is near, they tell me. I believe them. The fourth hits with a heat wave. My body swims in its own juices—

Gross!

—tears of pain streak my face. A spider scurries across
my toes. A rat runs, pauses at my ankle, and begins
to feast.

I do not know where I have staged this fictional suicide.

I allow it, partially because I lack the will to fight and
partially because I feel that if I move my body I will
fall apart. The fifth one crashes in, enraging my temples
and makes my forehead feel like it is imploding. I open
my mouth to scream and I feel my tongue fall out.

Which pill does that again? Is it Lexapro?

I am powerless. The sixth one sends me a surge of
energy, and I try to stand, using the wall for support,
feeling the splinters of wood tear the flesh from my face
and the cobwebs tangle in my eyelashes.

You got no tongue, Little Pam. That might overshadow the
irritation of spider homes by your eyeballs. And if not, it sounds
like you just left part of your face on a wall or something.

The seventh strikes me down again. I cannot move. I
cannot cry. At last I have succeeded. The eighth, ninth,
and tenth pull me and swirl me deeper into a darkness
more severe than the dismal atmosphere of the alcove I
had chosen to serve my hell.

God, I loved Nine Inch Nails.

The darker I fall, the less the pain. The screams
become softer, more pleasurable, whispers of peace.
I smile, and succumb to a world greater than any I've
ever experienced.

Oh, a happy ending!

I may not have done any drugs, but I knew what it felt like to want to die. I guess that's all you need to write something like this—a deep emptiness, that soul-crushing reality of being years away from freedom. Time slows to a horrible crawl during high school. As I type this, my own high school class is planning their reunion—their Facebook pages are going crazy over their excitement of the upcoming event—and all I can think is, *What did you do so differently that makes you want to go back?*

This is why we need two different high school reunions. There's the one for the people who have great memories from those four years—the ones who consider them the glory years. They can have their nametags and tables with centerpieces, reminiscing over drinks while flicking through endless photostreams of kids. They can crown another King and Queen. They can have one more night from their youth.

But I'll be a few cities over, in a bar, hosting the reunion for the ones who just want to make sure their friends from back then got out okay, that they're better now, happier, fell in love, or that their parents finally divorced. A check-in for the ones who moved far, far away from the town that didn't understand them. You know, we don't even all have to gather in the same place. Fuck it: it should be by Skype.

The anti-reunion. There to remind you how far you've come from the time in your life you had no idea how to be who you were supposed to be.

Being "Passionate"

I found an essay I wrote about *Roots*, and I think I only need to share the title to let you know how close I was to winning a Pulitzer.

Roots: It's Not About Gardening!

Was there anything at fifteen I didn't know the answer to? I think not!

This next piece I did actually share in public. Exactly once.

I am standing on a stage. I am fifteen. I am wearing a spandex unitard. It is white, with splatters of neon in pink and green. My hair is in a ponytail, high on my head. I have on more eye makeup than I've ever worn—or will ever wear—in my life. My hips have just come in, and I hate them, so I'm trying to make my legs look skinnier by keeping my arms stiff at my sides, my fingertips somehow sheltering my curves from view. I'm standing at attention like a slender soldier. Three girls in matching unitards are posed behind me, waiting.

I have memorized the following, which I recite to an audience attending…my Dance II recital.

Social Awareness

The earth is beautiful. Beautiful, but not perfect. We live in an age of war, AIDS, drugs, suicide, animal testing, divorce, murder, child abuse, incest, and rape. Where the ozone layer is being destroyed faster than we can calculate. Where every second another acre of the tropical rain forest is destroyed. Where every minute another species of plant or animal becomes extinct. Where there is a constant threat of nuclear war, toxic waste, natural disasters, oil spills, pollution, wars and the annihilation of the earth. Where homeless people crowd our streets and the insane are escaping, but we give money to build more weapons. Where only 15% of the entire population of Earth reads on a regular basis, and over a fourth of children drop out of school. Where gangs shoot and kill each other in your front yard, and where little girls are having little girls and boys of their own. Where famine is everywhere, and mutations and disease are infecting everything. All food is becoming bad for you, and everything is costing more.

Our dance reflects our feelings of separation, confusion, conformity and unity. Peace.

And then we danced to the first two minutes of Nine Inch Nails' "Head Like a Hole."

Now that's the kind of stuff you end indie movies with!

I knew it was very important to me to be passionate. Passionate people really lived life. They felt strongly and loved deeply and cared tremendously. Passionate people had adverbs in their blood, and I wanted to be full of that kind of vigor. I knew I had passion, but I struggled to find what I was truly passionate about. Love, sure. But I wanted to be the kind of person who made a difference when it came to *issues*.

One year I tried to be a vegetarian, but ultimately my parents grounded me until I ate meat. Then I wanted to protest the rodeo being in town, but my mom wouldn't drive me to a rally because she thought I was too young to be an activist. I resorted to sneaking "Fur is Murder" cards in the pockets of all the fur coats on the second floor of the Palais Royal. I gave money to Greenpeace and PETA and about three other animal rights groups that were most likely fronts for massive scams.

Nobody really cared about those things where I lived. It was so easy to dismiss vegans as hippies. It was frustrating because I was *really* angry about racism. It was everywhere, being both ignored and slightly encouraged. A kind of racism that's always been there, so it's accepted as the way things are going to be. Nobody saw a reason to think any differently. I mean, they stopped having slaves, what more do you want from them?

The Obligatory Poem About Cemetaries (But Also Racism)

Wood house standing
Puddled murky lawn
Telephone pole leaning
Small flowered path leads
to a field of silent souls
Words sum up centuries
Father, sister, lover.
Flesh symbolized by stone.
Souls of marble.
Spirits of posies and roses.
Tears of memory garden the paths
Smiles of rememberance [sic] keep the spirit alive
A monument to the life of death.
Words of praise make everyone beautiful.
Marble makes no color lines.
Stone shows no predjudice [sic].
Everyone is equally silent.
Living individually and equally.
But perfectly.
  —RIBON, MARCH 1992

"They're Looking For You."

Racism and prejudice became common themes in my journals because there was nowhere else to talk about them. I was the ultimate good girl, afraid of making waves, riding a school bus that regularly passed houses flying the following flags: USA, Texas, Confederacy, Klan. Back on my first day at that school, some stranger kid approached me at my locker. He got right in my face, examining it. "Blue eyes. Blonde hair. You'll be fine here. We won't bother you. White Power."

Before you dismiss all this as young kids being stupid because they were raised by assholes, know that a couple of them had beaten a Vietnamese boy to death right before I moved there. The assault had even been covered in my beloved *Sassy* magazine, complete with a photograph from the funeral. "I don't know what the big deal is," a kid on my bus said about the teenagers who were awaiting sentences at the time. "All they did was kill some gook."

My high school didn't celebrate Martin Luther King Day. Instead, we had the day off to reflect and appreciate Rodeo Day. That sounds like a punch line, but sadly, it is the truth. It also celebrated Slave Day, a yearly fund-raiser for the football team where the players would stand on an "auction block" in the cafeteria and be sold to the highest bidder. Once you owned your slave, you could do whatever you wanted with him. Often these boys were chained around the neck and dragged around the school. (Senior year even I participated in this tradition, but tried to go subversive—I dressed my nerdy valedictorian "slave" in bondage gear. (And no, I know that doesn't make it any better.))

It might still have Slave Day every year. I don't know. I still can't believe it wasn't an episode of *Friday Night Lights*, a show I couldn't watch when it first aired, as it was too close to going back to the years where every day I had to either shut up or defend myself. It reminds me of all the times I was too nervous to speak.

We moved to that town at the height of a Satanic Panic that caused the school district to create a shockingly offensive dress code. You couldn't wear black or red three days in a row, your hair had to be kept off your face, skirts had to land at the knee, and all symbols were banned except for the Christian cross, including the Star of David, which was considered "Satanic." I didn't attend a church, which was another strike against me. More than one friend was forced to stop hanging out with me, since I wasn't being "raised right."

I would have fantasies of staging a walkout to protest the dress code, but instead I diligently finished my World History exam. In my mind I was brave, holding a microphone in front of a gang of students who had HAD ENOUGH, who no longer wanted to be told what to do or what to think. But I felt useless being just a freshman, one who had no idea how to say anything that mattered to anyone. When I took my first stand back in my freshman year, my first bold declaration of Who I Was and What I Wouldn't Stand For, I started smaller than racism or fascism or elitism or religious prosecution. I announced to my family one night during dinner that I was going to abstain from dissecting a frog.

"They don't need to kill a frog for me," I said, probably with a mouth full of *steak au poivre*. "There are computer programs, pictures I could color in and label. Besides, I already dissected a frog in the seventh grade; I shouldn't have to do it again."

"You're dissecting a frog," my father said. "No further discussion. You're going to have to dissect lots of things if you want to be a doctor."

At the time it was still a general agreement between my parents that I would grow up to be one of those lawyerdoctors smart kids are supposed to want to be. (Although Mom had secret hopes I'd grow up to be a stand-up comedian in between my brain surgeon gigs.) "You might as well get used to the frogs," Dad added. "Because one day you're going to be cutting up cats."

"But I'm not studying to be a doctor right now. I'm in high school. I'll sit in the back and watch if I have to, but I'm not cutting up anything. I don't want something to have to die in order for me to pass Biology."

I must have thought I was so clever with that statement, but all I'd done was remind Dad of my Kryptonite.

"You're going to dissect that frog," he said. "I'm going to call the school and ask them if you did it. And if I find out you sat out of the lab, if they tell me you sat in the back or asked to draw something instead, I will tell them to give you an F. I will tell them to fail you because you didn't complete the assignment. Do I make myself clear?"

Dad ended a lot of his orders with that question, even though he always knew he had made himself crystal.

I was back in my room, furious that I couldn't skip frog dissection, furious that I had to cut my bangs because the school said they were considered "a distraction." (I'd worn my hair in a skater "flop," the dumbest haircut in the world, but I liked being able to hide behind something if I needed to just fucking disappear because I was fucking thirteen and shit was unfair.) I was sitting in my room with my notebook and a pen, wishing I was cool enough to have a zine or write for *Sassy*, but I was a nobody in a tiny town, and I was never, ever getting out of there for at least four years give or take a million, and so I had no choice but to start writing my own underground newspaper.

Welcome to My Slice of Insanity.

Okay, so what's this? This is my way to say what I want to say. This is also your way to hear what I have to say. It's also your way to say what you have to say. This is called free expression. Say it with me now, "Free expression." It's the American form of anarchy. Because now and then we all need to raise a little hell. And that, kiddies, is what I'm here for. Let the games begin.

Oh, God. "Kiddies." It's like I'm sort of trying to be Stephen King but I'm also clearly Christian Slater in *Pump Up the Volume* and also kind of Eric Bogosian in *Talk Radio* while still trying to be Jane Pratt and it's all coming out as the wrong kind of condescending. (And maybe also Dana Carvey's Church Lady?) My idols were a weird mix at that time of comedians, journalists, and magicians. I mean it: there's a Penn Jillette essay in *Penn & Teller's Cruel Tricks For Dear Friends* that I basically ripped off in a million ways for the next five years (including in that elevator awkwardica earlier).

I guess I was satisfied with that intro enough that I moved on to what every proper underground newspaper needs:

Table of Contents

Are you kidding? A "table of contents" makes strict guidelines of what I have to say, what you have to read. It states what I have to say and how long it can be. No way. Uh uh. Free expression doesn't have rules. And neither do I. I write what I want to write when I want to write for how long I want to write. I might write a paragraph on recycling. I might write a 200 page article on pocket lint. So be it.

Yeah! *Fuck yeah, so be it! Read my lint-thoughts, bitches!*
Then I really got to work on writing what I wanted to write when I wanted to write what I wrote how I wrote for how long to be writing.

The Dress Code

I guess the topic that everyone is waiting for me to address is the dress code. Okay. These are my main problems.

1) Boy's hair rule
2) skirts/shorts rule
3) school damaging hair

My reasons:

1) I don't see why a guy can't wear his hair any longer than a girl can. I mean, as long as he washes it. I don't want a nest of roaches in front of me in Chem class. But then again, some guys look <u>really</u> good with long hair. Hair is one of the few ways humans have to express themselves physically. And for high school teenagers with a dress code, it may very well be the only way.

2) This rule has gotten out of hand. I have seen girls get sent to change when their skirt was 2 inches above the knee. But if a long-legged blonde wears a skirt 7 inches above the knee, male authority figures seem not to notice. Now I'm not saying that all girls should have knee-length skirts, I'm just saying that the officials should make up their minds and punish based on the clothes, not the one wearing them.

3) My main gripe about this one is I don't get it. I don't care how sharp one's liberty spikes are, they aren't going to scrape the paint off the gym walls.

Man, I wish I'd started with "Jewish People Aren't Satantic." I guess I wanted to ease my way into anarchism, just get people used to my snarky voice before I exposed the true hypocrisies of the school's rules.

Another problem was when I tried to write something from my heart about how upset I was about racism, it often came out like this:

My Asian eyes are small but there. I am not blind to the world around me.

I see the stares.

I see the child on his knees, hands like praying, bowing and rocking and gabbering nonsense in some teasing way.

I don't pray like that.

IN MY DEFENSE!—I scribbled all over that as soon as I finished, clearly knowing it was shit.

I went back to writing what I *knew* I was right about. I wanted to write about something that didn't get into messy religious debates that made parents shelter their children from me. I didn't want to engage in dialogue that could result in me hearing someone say the N-word. I didn't want to have to hide from the Klan. I wanted my writing to be important on a nation-wide scale. I had Things To Say about America! Things I learned because I had a subscription to *Rolling Stone*!

> A decision was made during the past school year that built my patriotism back up almost to what it once was. The trial to decide whether the 2 Live Crew's As Nasty As They Wanna Be was obscene—and should be banned— finally ended with a decision in the band's favor.

Not *at* my school. That's confusing, even to me. Nobody at my high school was asked to give an opinion on 2 Live Crew. (Other than the boy who wanted to pop my cherry to the dulcet tones of "Me So Horny.")

> The fact that this trial had to go all the way to the Supreme Court is what frightens me. We as Americans are supposed to have the Constitutional right of free speech, and the freedom to listen to what we choose. When the government steps in and takes things away from us "for our own good", eventually we will be sheltered from everything and we will no longer live in a democracy. It will be Hitler's dream revisited.

I was years ahead of troll culture, just itching for a comment section to ruin.

> Tipper Gore, the PMRC, Jessie Helms and any other authority figure that has been trying to drill into our heads that music can hurt you, books can corrupt,

television warps and sex is disgusting, has the power to make that dream a reality. To take an image away from a group of people because you do not feel it is beautiful is wrong. It is unconstitutional. It is unjust. It is unspeakable. It is unAmerican. [*sic*]

This horror will not stop once the last 2 Live Crew album is trashed, or the last Robert Mapplethorpe artwork is burned, or the last starving "controversial" artist has conformed to finding a new angle to draw a fucking [*that word is crossed out in red pen*] bowl of fruit. It will not stop when the last copy of *The Catcher in the Rye* or *Huckleberry Finn* is banned from school bookshelves because of strong language.

True story: I checked *A Clockwork Orange* out of the school library after Super Mario Brothers Boy mentioned it in passing (which meant I had to read it immediately so I had a whole new thing to talk to him about with passion and importance). But for the first time in the history of reading, this novel didn't make much sense. The story would jump and skip; whole sections seemed to have nothing to do with each other. It wasn't a very long book, so I couldn't understand what I was supposed to understand.

"What do you mean you don't get it?" SMB Boy asked me. "It's not that hard. Let me see it."

I handed him the hardcover copy. His eyes went wide. "Where's the rest of it?"

He flipped through the pages to show me how the book had been heavily censored. Chapters were missing. Pages had been ripped from the spine.

I was outraged. I was insulted. I was...*inspired to take to pen*!

It will not stop once the last Judas Priest album stops spinning, or when the last underground newspaper is shredded. By then the wheel of destruction will be spinning so rapidly that nothing will be spared.

The book censoring was a continued sore spot for me, because the school would allow a student to opt out of any required reading if the parents objected to the material for religious reasons. This means when we were supposed to read *Brave New World*, a large portion of my English class opted to read the apocalyptic sci-fi novel *Alas, Babylon* instead, because *Brave New World* discussed birth control, a forbidden topic. "But *Brave New World* is about exactly what your parents are making you do!" I shouted, to nobody, because nobody wanted to listen.

The next time I shouted to a classroom filled with insanity, I made sure to be heard.

It was my senior year AP American History class, where a considerable amount of time was devoted to teaching us that slavery "wasn't that bad." An actual teacher stood at the front of the classroom and said that. With her mouth. Using her voice.

All around me my classmates were taking notes, scribbling something like *Slavery = not that bad* and after four years of this bullshit, after enough time spent with the gleefully outspoken troublemaker SMB Boy, after watching the latest wave of fake Skinheads in my school shave their heads and carry around copies of *Mein Kampf* that they'd never read, I couldn't stop myself from raising my hand.

"Are you really trying to tell us that slavery wasn't that bad, or are you waiting for one of us to question you?"

This teacher always found me to be a little annoying. It started with a project on the Bill of Rights, where I spent much of my presentation on the First Amendment emphasizing how this country was founded on the concept of religious freedom, so maybe some people could stop leaving Chick tracts inside my locker. The teacher interrupted my rant about free speech to call me, most condescendingly, "My little flower child."

Questioning her judgment on calling slavery "not that bad" elicited an enormous eye roll.

"I mean, those people didn't know how to read or write," she said. "So they weren't going to be able to make it on their own, anyway. They were lucky to have slave owners, who housed them and fed them, even when they were still having children. And that's just more mouths to feed. There had to have been a certain level of care, otherwise they weren't going to be good workers."

Something inside of me snapped.

"EVERYBODY IN THIS ROOM NEEDS TO READ *ROOTS*." I shouted it, and then I couldn't stop. "READ *ROOTS*. GET A COPY. READ IT. YOU NEED TO READ IT. THIS IS WRONG, WHAT SHE'S SAYING IS WRONG."

I don't know how everybody got the memo on the fastest way to shut me down, but the teacher got all gaspy and hand fluttery as she stammered, "Well, I am just going to report this outburst to the principal's office!"

"Go ahead!" I shouted, so sure in the fact that this time nobody could tell me I was wrong. This time I would gladly serve any detention (*oh God, please, no, I've never had detention*) or punishment (*but please no, please don't call my dad oh God*) because I knew I was right.

So I added: "Suck my dick!"

Those three words I didn't shout until the teacher left the room. Everybody was staring at me, mouths all huge with the O shape. I didn't care. "Seriously. Read *Roots*."

The American History teacher never came back to the classroom. Eventually, the bell rang. The next day she went on as if nothing had ever happened. Our exchange was never brought up again.

> Total conformity will have seeped through the veins of America and anyone trying to stop this deadly cycle will be run over and swept under the governmental rug. Big Brother is at hand…but this trial decision helped to stall him.

> We must do something about censorship. Now.

> Fight censorship.

I knew my underground newspaper was great. It was fantastic. I was going to have a huge audience, a school filled with rabid fans who would all want to know, "*Who is this brave, new voice of our generation? Who is this keen social observer who turns an unflinching mirror on our society? And most importantly: when will she write more? WHEN WILL SHE WRITE MORE??"*

All of that could happen once I figured out how to distribute. I didn't have access to a computer, nor a photocopier. I didn't even know where to find a mimeograph. No job, no car, no money, and a standing obligation to watch my little sister after school—the odds were stacked against me. I briefly thought about hand-copying a couple hundred times, but that was precious time I'd spend reprinting that would be better served writing.

I must have complained about my lack of a printing press to the boy my parents hated so much, the one with the disposable income, because the next thing I know there's now a whole group of kids who are "starting an underground paper." There was a secret meeting, one I wasn't able to attend because I didn't have a car, nor was I allowed to attend secret meetings at the house of the boy whom my parents were terrified I'd start dating again if I came within fifty feet. Missing the informative introductory meeting meant I was relegated to the section known as "and other contributors." I might as well have been their overseas reporter. The underground newspaper was my baby, my creation, and now I was barely a participant. I was pretty sure they weren't even going to use my Table of Contents!

Since high school kids are mostly poseur assholes, some other group of kids found out there were plans for an underground newspaper, and decided *they* were going to make an underground newspaper. But these kids had money so they were able to get an issue printed before my editorial staff could finish distributing assignments. (I know it sounds like I'm describing some shitty episode of *My So-Called Life*, but I'm not making any of this up.) So the rich kids got their issue off the press and distributed it all over the school. It's really subpar stuff, just gossip and teacher-bashing and not one mention of fighting the power. Nobody's calling anyone "Kiddies" and there's nobody trying to be the voice of a generation. There's no Christian Slater in the night. There's just a bunch of lame jokes and slanderous rumors. And a crossword. A fucking crossword.

(That's genius, why didn't I think of a crossword?)

I'm walking down the hallway a couple of days later and this big guy in a denim jacket with patches all over it stops me with his pudgy hand. "Hey," he says, eyes darting around nervously. "They're cracking down on the paper. They're bringing people in for questioning. The Richies are pinning it on us and now they're looking for you."

And then he walked away.

Suddenly my life was exactly how I'd always dreamed it would be and also the most terrifying thing I'd ever experienced. I was part of the underground movement, part of the "problem," part of the change I wanted to see, but also *what if they called my dad what if I get grounded for this or worse—what is the weird punishment Dad will dish out for an underground paper? Will he make me start a paper route? Will he ground me from paper? What if he grounds me from paper? HOW WILL I WRITE? HOW WILL I TAKE TESTS? Oh God oh God what if they take me in and it's on my PERMANENT RECORD?*

"I'm out!"

I remember shouting that at a lunchroom table, trying to contain my passion, trying not to enjoy this moment because I was serious. "If they call me in I won't say anything, but I'm out."

They hadn't even printed an issue, and their current plans for one contained exactly zero things I had written, so it was really brave of me to pull out when I did.

"Okay," they said.

"Don't use any of my stuff, I mean it."

"Okay. We're probably not going to do it, anyway."

"Okay, but still."

"Okay."

And then I sat down. "Their paper was so lame," I said.

"I know. So lame."

"Ours was going to be so much cooler!"

"So much cooler."

Since this was a Friday, our underground paper died by the end of the day's final bell.

I believe I wrote the following hoping there was still a chance that one day everyone in my school would read it.

31, March, 1991

She couldn't take it any longer.

Every nerve in her body shot out simultaneously charging her straight up into the air, her body rigid and her eyes flaming.

She pushed aside the small crowd of people ahead of her—probably with more force than she intended—and walked with determination down the long row of bleachers, to the open gymnasium plain beneath her.

Her steps were rhythmic, her breathing was rapid. Fists clenched and near her sides she completed her descent and as she reached the bottom she lifted her head and took a deep breath.

She could still turn back. Not many had noticed her outburst. She could return to her small circle of friends with a dumb excuse about not being able to see someone on the other side of the gym or that she thought a teacher was calling her.

Not this time.

She wasn't going to be among the silent majority this time. She wasn't going to sit there this time and let this madness continue.

She quickened her pace and approached the microphone, which at the moment was occupied by a cheerleader who was bouncing and cheering to an elementary beat, ponytail swinging and skirt swirling to reveal muscular legs and underwear boldly striped in school colors: black and white.

The cheerleader noticed her now, and stopped bouncing. She opened her hideously painted mouth to form some form of protest, but it was of no use. She was shoved aside, causing an uproar from the bleachers, and an open space for a new speaker. One who had something important to say.

The cheering continued even as the cheerleader ran off crying. Four thousand teenagers were cheering, stomping, screaming, singing, arguing and almost changed the speaker's mind.

Almost.

Clutching the microphone in her quivering right hand, she opened her mouth to speak. A clicking noise formed in her mouth, and she gave a slight cough to clear it. She looked around at the zoo of youth around her and began her plea.

"Please listen to me."

Her friends sat down and stared at her, a few made small remarks, trying to sound intelligent and humorous, but were silenced by others. Some continued their chaos, still making their own noise, until they noticed the silence of the majority, and they too sat down and focused their eyes on one young female who stood before them.

"This is wrong," she began. Her voice stammered, and she began to rock back and forth, transferring her weight from one foot to the other—a nervous habit she had for years. She caught herself, cleared her throat and started again.

"I'm sick and tired of it and it is wrong." She closed her eyes, hoping it would calm her nerves, but still feeling eight thousand probing eyes staring into her.

"You may not know who I am, but that should not matter. What I have to say should be said by everyone, and should be thought by all."

"Yeah, whatever baby," came a voice from deep within the bleachers on her left. A few laughs followed.

"I have something I have to say," she tried to continue, but a principal came toward her, trying to usher her off the court. He touched her shoulder—

"Come on," he said, his face blank of expression, as if he was expecting something like this and that it was an everyday occurrance [sic].

"Don't touch me," she said, causing a few cheers from her captive audience.

"Let's go," the man said again with an aggressive tone of voice. He jerked her arm toward him and tried to pull her away.

"I said let go of me!" she yelled, her words echoing through the gymnasium.

The principal drew her in close and placed his hand over the top of the microphone. He put his flaming face beside her ear and hissed, "Look, n*$$#r, if you don't cooperate there's going to be a lot more trouble here than just expulsion."

His hand did not posses the power to silence his words, and the student body was an uproar, the right side— the black students shouted insults and obsenities [*sic*], and threw obscene gestures toward the man. The far left—the whites—began applause. The near left—other minorities—remained silent.

"Mr. Orland, go fuck yourself," she said softly and walked back to the middle of the floor.

Two teachers pulled back the outraged principal and looked up to the girl with the microphone.

"This has got to stop," she said, without a hint of nervousness in her voice. "This cannot continue. Racism is wrong. It's so wrong that I can't even begin to understand the reason why it would be acceptable. It's stupid, is what it is. Hating someone for what is on the outside makes no sense. It makes no fucking sense at all."

Okay, so that's the second time I've censored these letters and stories. I hope you forgive me for both. This book is permanent, and I don't know if I can handle my father discussing my mother's sexual appetite, or the one time I wrote out the n-word living in foreverness.

Out of curiosity, I just looked up the current required summer reading for gifted seniors at my old high school. It's *Narrative of the Life of Frederick Douglass*. And now I'm crying, really, honestly crying, because a small piece of Little Pam finally found a happy ending.

The Confession...

I worship not to Gods—
My superiors are literary.
A pen becomes my cross.
My rosary? Sheets of paper.
My place of worship changes
From a museum to a library.
I am silent in either.
Respecting the displays of talent.
Remnants of souls make me
Who I am.
Forcing me to reflect on what
I once was.
I feel reborn.
These words and images mold me.
I give my confession to the chilled marble steps.
Forgive me, for it has been too long since my last
confession.
Twice I doubted my worth.
Three times my strength has faltered.
Once I pretended I was someone that I wasn't.
Four times I tried to conform.
I lay my face against the tile
Its energy feeds me.
I am stripped of my sin.
And handed a pen
For my emotions to encompass.
I need not deities from heaven.

I only need the wisdom to know myself
To trust myself
To laugh at foolish choices
Even if they are my own.
The doors close
As do my eyes.
An internal amen.

Part Four

Getting Serious

I Never Dated Jim Morrison, But I Think I Wanted The Guy I Was Seeing To Feel Like I Thought Of Him That Way

1 April 1992

You are my everything. You make the fires blaze around me, encircling me in a heatwave of emotion. A calming, soothing frenzy. You make the air thick with a gentle passion.

You are sounding an awful lot like the sky in Los Angeles, so I should probably take some Allegra before we keep kissing.

You are my strength when chaos arises. You are my idol when I'm stripped of my cheap shelters.

You are hopefully able to explain to me what that sentence means. I'm sure it sounds awesome when you're almost seventeen. And you're at a Renaissance Faire.

You are my light when I'm blind with confusion and sorrow. You summon the gods of beauty. You invite the gods of sex as you peel off your patched pieces of erotica and stand before me—exposed as who you really are.

You are the sun, I am the moon, you are the words, I am a vomiting thesaurus. What the fuck kind of erotica has a patched piece? Nobody wants *used* erotica. And if he's peeling it…am I describing stitched-up leather, like some kind of kinky bondage? Or am I describing a key moment from *Silence of the Lambs*?

More than flesh, you are blood and fears and tears and anger and screams and beating heart. You chase me. My senses reel. My soul spins. A valley between us, chases are mental; I cannot reach to touch—only see, only feel, only real.

Only me.

I need a shower.

April 5, 1992
[I am now seventeen.]

I think this is the story of me kissing a dead person. Either that or I'm breaking into boys' homes and assaulting their lips and arms while they sleep.

> She moves toward him—silently—so as not to arouse his resting state. She stares at his undisturbed beauty in awe. Her eyes touch him in places where her fingers cannot. She caresses his face with her sight, giving little kisses to his closed eyes, the bridge of his nose, the tip of his chin. She lingers around his lips, when her will power begins to crumble. She sinks to her knees and puts her hands on his arm. She leans down and kisses him lightly, briefly on his lips. She brushes her mouth across his cheek (the softness of his skin tingles the nerves of her lips) and again rests her mouth on him, this time on his earlobe. He is the vision of perfection, a stunning beauty who she would die for. She notices her time runs low, and she pulls the crumpled white flower from her bag. She places it beside him, kisses his forehead in a brief final emotion, and runs away, brushing her tears aside in haste.

If I had to make a real guess, I would say this is a story about seeing a boy asleep on the floor of some break room or backstage during rehearsal and while he was asleep I thought about kissing him and instead I left him a flower because I am nothing if not a dork.

The Very Last Time I Ever
Rode a School Bus

It's already the most dangerous part of any school day, riding a bus. That thing doesn't have a seatbelt anywhere to be found and kids usually spend most of the trip standing up or walking around.

I've already mentioned my various crushes and semi-sexual experiences sitting on that bus, as well as the time a Skinhead kid brushed off a hate crime. But I haven't told you yet that the day I was trying to get Mr. Snausage to take my virginity, Super Mario Brothers Boy was literally getting his head bashed in on that bus. He'd gotten into a fight over who could sit where. These other kids beat him up, and the bus driver told SMB Boy to get off her bus, as he was "bleeding all over her seats." He needed stitches. (Understandably, he still regrets not bringing up a lawsuit.)

My house was about a mile from a video rental store, and I often walked the short distance by myself to return or rent tapes. One time I was on my way to return two movies (*Pink Floyd The Wall* and Monty Python's *The Meaning of Life*. I really don't have to tell you anything else to describe exactly who I was or what I was wearing that day. Just those two tapes in my hand), when about halfway through my walk, a car pulled up in front of me. I recognized the boys inside from my bus, but I didn't know them well. "Get in," they said. "We're headed to that video store, too."

"No, that's okay," I said. "I'm almost there." I'm no dummy.

"But we want to rent those movies, and we don't want to stand there waiting for you to return them. This'll be faster."

"They probably have other copies."

"You know they don't." They didn't. I knew they didn't.

"No, just let me walk. I'll meet you there."

"Come on, this'll be faster."

"No."

"Just do it, bitch, come on!"

I honestly don't remember if I got into their car or they pulled me into their car, but my next memory is that I am inside their car and I am scared shitless because it is instantly clear they are not taking me to the video store.

"Take me home, then," I say. "You can have the videos."

They just laugh. They see how scared I am and they laugh. "Why are you scared?" they ask. "We aren't fucking doing anything to you. You're just in our car. Calm the fuck down, what's wrong with you?"

And they're right, but they're wrong, and I'm scared but they're just some asshole kids who ride my bus so why the fuck am I so scared? They can't do anything. Right?

"Just take me home."

Home, where my sister is. Where my parents aren't. But home, where I can lock the door and stay inside and never leave the house again.

"Okay, fine. But we're keeping the tapes."

They knew exactly where I lived since I rode their bus. They drove up to my house and pulled into the driveway. I jumped out of the car and ran inside, the videotapes still in my hand. I slammed the front door.

"Go to your room!" I shouted at my twelve-year-old sister as I locked the bottom lock, then the deadbolt.

"What's happening?"

"Just go to your room." I run to the kitchen. I grab the phone. I dial 9. I dial 1. I wait.

"Pamie, they're coming through the window!"

I see my little sister beating the back of this large boy who is climbing through the front window, the venetian blinds crinkling and crumbling, bending in a way that will definitely get us in trouble. That's what I was thinking—*We're busted now, Dad's going to see those blinds*—that's what I was thinking as I hung up the phone and grabbed a knife from the wooden block and screamed, "GET OUT OF MY HOUSE!"

The boys just laughed. Again. I'm constantly hilarious to them. The taller one came closer. "Cut me," he said. "Do it. I dare you. I dare you to do it. What the fuck are you going to tell them?"

I don't remember his face anymore. I remember his blonde hair, how he was tall and angled, everything jutting in weird places. He had bad skin and a smirk that overtook his features. Just a snarl sitting on top of a lanky body.

I could hear the other boy, the heavier one, down the hall, in my bedroom, rifling through my things. I heard my drawers opening, change rattling.

"Get out of my house," I said, my sister behind me, my hand trembling, heart just about stopped. "Get out!"

They left, but not before they filled their arms with things they swiped from my room, including a journal and a jar filled with all my money.

I immediately called Super Mario Brothers Boy and told him what happened. Because, I guess, that's what you do when you don't want to get in trouble for having boys over. I didn't know who else to call. My parents would have been angry, the police would have told my parents, and nobody else would care what just happened.

Super Mario Brothers Boy came over and sat with us. He made a few calls. Friends of his friends knew the boys, and someone got them to drive back and return some of my things. I remember SMB Boy pacing the driveway as he negotiated the terms of getting my money back.

My parents saw the window, of course, and they were understandably livid. My father was angrier than I'd seen him in a long time. He said what I'd done was stupid, and that I'd handled it all wrong. That I don't call a boy I like when something like that happens; I call the police. That I never get into a car with any boy like that, even someone I know.

"Do you realize you and your sister could have been killed? Or worse?"

I sometimes had these mental splits when my father was yelling at me. Part of me would be there, truly there in the moment where Dad's red faced, standing over me as I sat hunched in his plush recliner, the one he had me sit in the night he wouldn't let me sleep. I was listening, feeling scared for how mad he was, worried that he'd never stop being angry, knowing that the more he raged, the worse the punishment was going to be when he finally stopped ranting.

But the rest of me would be momentarily amused at his choice of words. He just said there was something that could happen that was "worse" than death. I remember so clearly my father's face when he yelled that at me, because he lost his breath on "Or worse." He lost his breath because he started to cry and he left the room. And then I knew what he thought was worse. And how terrifying it must be to raise a teenage girl.

It was the first time I ever saw my father look scared. It was the first time I ever saw him realize he could be powerless.

When I got on the bus the next morning there were a few snickers as I walked down the aisle. A pair of my panties dangled over my seat, pinned in the windowframe.

That's the last time I ever rode a school bus.

Months later when I first became friends with the boy with the disposable income, I told him this story. He told one of his friends, a big guy respected by everybody in the school, a guy who didn't really know me but cared a lot about justice. He walked over to those guys at their locker, leaned in, and said, "I heard you fucked with my friend Pam Ribon. You'd better fix it." The videotapes were returned the next day.

His name was Marshall. What a great name for an anonymous hero.

Ode to a New Journal:

7 April 1992

Where do I begin? I long to tell you everything, to share with you my innermost dreams and ideas.

I want to laugh with you, watching the candlelight dance in your eyes as your hand clasps mine. I want to cry with you, having you hold my heaving shoulders when the world becomes too much to bear. I want you to share your fears with me—we'll hide in our secret magickal monster-protecting fort holding hands and stealing kisses, forgetting the existance [*sic*] of a real world; only we two matter now. I need you, and I wish so that you needed me. How do I need you? you ask.

Where do I begin?

May 7, 1992

It all ends soon. The laughter bouncing in this room will echo forever in the halls in memory. Now will never be again.

I will wait until the end of this piece to tell you what I'm writing about. See if you can guess.

We have created the strongest relationships that perhaps we will ever have. When looking back on these years we will remember not the examinations of our knowledge, but the smiles and tears we shared from our souls. Love was built here. Trust was built here. Warmth was built here. An unforgettable feeling of safety circulates in this room. Stronger than the Three Musketeers. An unforgettable tribe of individuals. Crazy.

You're wrong. That was about my Yearbook class.

I am Pretty Sure I Sent This in to at Least One College Application, Which Means I May Have Sent This to Yale.

When I was seven, I would lock myself in a closet with a stack of paper and a large, clunky typewriter and write stories until I could no longer keep my eyes open. Ever since I can remember I've had a certain knack for writing; the words would always come easily, my grammar and spelling were almost always perfect. I can only recall two occasions where I've scored as low as a "B" on an essay.

Now I sit amongst a sea of crumpled papers at a definite loss for words. I do not think that my mental block is because this essay is for a college, or even that it decides my future. This essay is difficult because it has to answer the question, "Who am I?"

I am not sure where to begin. Do I start with awards I have won or classes I have taken?

This is much easier for me from now on if I just imagine that this is B. J. Novak from *The Office* talking, instead of me. Not the character he played on the show. Actual B. J. Novak. This is what I imagine he sounds like, even when he's like, buying fifteen items or less and someone has asked if he has his Ralph's card with him.

Do I first talk about my background (how this is my twelfth school or my endless string of Gifted and Talented classes?)

Should I mention that I was in the Latin Club and the Chess Club or should I downplay those and accent my efforts as Vice President of Drama Club or Assistant Editor of Yearbook staff? I am not sure if it is bragging to mention my Best Actress, All-Star Cast and Honorable Mention All-Star Cast awards in last year's U.I.L. Competitions.

I have no way of knowing whether the fact that I received the Best Actress award from my 5A school last year makes a difference in how people perceive me. A thousand questions run through my head because I am not sure how to present myself accurately.

I do know that I am friendly, hard working and organized. I make friends very easily (you have to when you move every six months) and I am very trusting. I have an open mind and I enjoy learning about anything and everything I can.

Am I applying for a college or a three-way?

For example, this year I made the Academic Decathalon [*sic*] team and we are currently studying in preparation for our regional meet. I have always been very ambitious: I am planning on a double major. Last year I discovered my passion for acting. I always thought that I could do it, but my proof was in the fact that I was moved from a Theatre I class to a Theatre III class on teacher recommendation, in the 1st place awards I have received, and most importantly in the applause (and standing ovations!) that I and the rest of the cast hear after every performance.

In high school I have discovered the highs and lows of love and romance, learned how to be a good listener, earned a new respect for my parents and teachers, and discovered the priceless value of friendship.

Being shifted from school to school often as a little girl I have been frequently asked the question, "Who are you?" I used to be unable to answer this question; I used to be afraid to speak my mind. When I was two, I taught myself how to read. I was quite the novelty in kindergarden [*sic*] class, often leading the storytime sessions. As I got older my abilities became less impressive to the other children, and they began to resent my talents.

Now at seventeen I am more confidant [*sic*] and proud. I dislike telling people about the awards I have won. Over the past four years I have grown from a clutzy, giggly freshman to a strong, talented woman who can accomplish anything I want as long as my will is there. I can and will make a difference.

Who Wants Honey

"I really do care about you."

He pushed his dyed-black hair out of his eyes as he spoke.

"His heart is as false as his hair," something told me.

I should have listened.

At some point I reconnected with School Bus Boy. I can't remember if he was doing tech for a show I was in, or we ran into each other at a cast party. I just know this was sometime before I left for college, possibly in the summer. This story sounds better in the summer weeks before I moved away to Austin, so let's place it there.

School Bus Boy hadn't changed much since our early high school days on the bus, at least physically. He was still on the small side, sported a Johnny Depp-load of jewelry over white T-shirts and baggy jeans. His fingernails, however, were filed in a less vampiric way, probably because he had reached the age where he needed to keep an actual job. He asked if I'd like to hang out. "Spend some time together." He said it like that, "*Spend some time together*," like he was reading from the first page of a handbook called *Nothing But Shitty Lines To Say To Girls*.

I said yes. Yes, I would like to hang out.

I immediately began plotting my revenge.

I followed the directions to his place to pick him up. Once inside the small apartment he shared with his mother, I had that disorienting feeling that often happened when I was younger, when my world was so small and my focus so inward that I had to be reminded how everybody has a different life. It was such a bizarre concept to me. Why wouldn't everybody have a very similar life with very similar goals? It just made sense that everybody would have a sibling and live in a house where both parents worked. I assumed everybody wanted good grades so they could go to college. Who wouldn't want to go to college? The first time I even heard about someone thinking about not going to college, my mind was blown. "*So, are you just going to be a drug dealer?*"

Television may have had something to do with this weird perception. Every kid on every show was basically the same, except for that one who was a pretty little robot. My terror at not getting into college was clearly fueled by the PSAs that aired during those shows. "*I thought nobody ever said they wanted to be a junkie when they grew up. But you're kind of doing that right now! Go to college!*"

I had little experience with single mothers. Whenever I was at the house of one, everything always seemed more adult. Without the heavy weight of a father somewhere in the house, imposing draconian rules while maintaining an ulcerative sense of order, to me these homes had an exciting tremble of freedom. They seemed so civilized, so peaceful.

I had even less experience with kids who lived in apartments instead of houses. School Bus Boy's life was, to me, as different as if I was actually living inside an episode of *21 Jump Street* and I was the undercover narc trying to charm my way into a new group of kids. "*So this is your living room and also where your mom sleeps? Fascinating. I mean, yes, of course. Me too. We're the same, you and I. Do you have a place where you like to keep your drugs and marijuana?*"

Seeing the home life of School Bus Boy made me falter just a bit from my mission, so I had to remind myself that no matter how romantic or scrappy his life with his mom might be, it didn't excuse how he treated me.

We went to my house to pick up my Smashing Pumpkins CD. *Siamese Dream* had just come out so we needed it, as we couldn't imagine doing anything that night without that new album playing. Sometimes I miss that age in my life when a CD could be that important, that it could be something I couldn't go another minute without hearing. Music could once define the night's path, tell us how to feel, or simply give us a reason to make out.

I was awkward at being a teenage girl, and that is why I had a pair of handcuffs strapped to my wrought-iron daybed. Because I couldn't even do a hint of kink without dorking it up, most people didn't know that they were actually trick handcuffs, leftovers from my magician phase. There was a safety latch so they could come undone whenever I wanted, but I always made it seem like those cuffs didn't have a key, so if we used them, it was going to be serious.

School Bus Boy had already started the CD and "Cherub Rock" was playing (*Freak out / And give in / Doesn't matter what you believe in*) as he leaned back on my bed. He stared at me as he grabbed the bed frame, his hands on either side of the cuffs. (*Stay cool /And be somebody's fool this year…*) Then he looked at me, making his eyes go all Blue Steel as he said, "I will be your fool."

I laughed. I accidentally laughed, but it was just too much, it was so literal and I knew how this night was going to end. I laughed because for the first time ever, and maybe ever again, at this moment I was looking at a boy who was looking at me and he was interested in me and I didn't care. I was actively disengaged. He was my science experiment.

I laughed, but I wasn't happy. I suddenly felt like I had been wasting so much time, so many months and years of pining, so much heart-wringing, over someone like this. Not School Bus Boy specifically—he was just playing an awkward game as he tried to figure out his odds on getting a handjob that night—but all of the romance I'd been searching for, all of the *I love you need you want you* passion I'd assumed was coming my way just as soon as I'd found The One.

School Bus Boy offering to be my fool made something click. What I wanted wasn't possible in high school, because I had become…*a woman.*

I was a woman scorned. By this boy.

We went to a parking lot, where we kissed for a while, long enough that it didn't make sense that we were still only kissing. Long enough that any two teens with this kind of intensity combined with the ticking clock of a curfew would have started moving towards taking off some clothes.

But I didn't. I kept him outside of the car, standing up, asking me for more. I made him beg me for more. I made him say it, made him tell me what he wanted, in detail, tell me what he'd like to do, why he needed me, why it had to be me, why he craved me. I made him tell me that it hurt not to have me; that he wanted to taste me. That he wanted to touch me. I made him beg.

And then I said no.

I got in my car and I drove away and I never talked to School Bus Boy again.

Not even to write him an apology.

June 21, 1992

Ah-HA! I KNEW Mom was wrong. *This* is the story about the cat. That means that other one…well, I probably gave it to a boy. And that means I really did write a story about my cat. And it's this.

> …*Murray's Monologue*…

> Veronica held the cat in her arms; her gentle strokes calmed her deeper and deeper into sleep.

> "Good night, Murray," she murmured. "I love you."

> She felt a bite on her cheek. Veronica opened her eyes to darkness, a rumbling was on her chest. Her tension eased when she realized it was her cat demanding affection.

> "Murray, you stupid cat," she said as she scratched him under his chin. "You scared me."

> "Listen to me."

> The sound of the voice caused Veronica to jump in her bed, emiting [*sic*] a yelp of fear. The voice spoke again.

> "Calm down, Veronica. This is a dream." Murray's mouth formed these words perfectly. His voice was low and soothing. She relaxed, feeling herself sink deeper into her bed.

"Listen, there are some things I need to tell you, so shut up until I'm done, okay?"

Veronica's eyes, which were now adjusted to the darkness, were wide with surprise and astonishment. She managed a speechless nod.

"I've watched you grow up from a stupid little girl to a beautiful, intelligent young woman. You've made something of yourself. I'm proud of you. I just want to make sure you know this before you go off to college.

Listen, Veronica. There's going to be a lot of things that are going to try to affect you, even try to hurt you. Don't let them. Be strong. Don't change the beautiful person that you are."

"Murray," Veronica interrupted. "How do you know this?"

"I'm going to let you in on a little secret about pets: we're guardian angels. We are sent here to protect you. In my last life I was an exterminator."

Veronica laughed. "No wonder you like to eat bugs."

"Anyway, when you come back as an animal, you lose your ability to verbally communicate, that's why I sit on your lap when you cry, bite your ankle when I'm hungry, rub your shin when I've missed you, or wait at the window for you to come home.

You leave for college tomorrow. My job is done. I don't have much time left to tell you that I love you. Goodbye, Veronica."

"Murray, you act like you'll never see me again. It's only college, for Christ's sake."

"Watch your language."

Veronica sighed. "I think I liked it better when you were silent. Can I end this dream now, Murray?"

Murray looked down. A tear fell down his face. "As you wish," he whispered.

When Veronica woke in the morning she found Murray's dead body at the foot of her bed.

See? Now *that's* how you write a cat story.

Missing the Missing

This is folded and ripped out of a notebook, so I know—I AM POSITIVE—that this is a first draft and the second draft was sent to its intended target.

> I lay here in misery. Isolation. My mind is chaos. My breath quick. My soul restless.

At first I thought this letter was written because I had been grounded.

> My first night without you.
> The first of many.

But then I read those lines and I knew. This was when Super Mario Brothers Boy was sent to live with his father.
Fifteen hundred miles away.
To say I was devastated is an understatement.

> Before I was so happy I couldn't even touch a pen. Now despair has sent the words flowing. Every word an attempt at a kiss, a touch, an embrace—that can't quite reach you—>

> —I wish it could. I wish to God it could.

That arrow really is there, and I wish you could see it. I wish to God you could see it.

It happened very quickly, Super Mario Brothers Boy leaving. Or at least it felt like one day he was there and the next he was gone. Unreachable. Ripped from me. I'm sure it had something to do with his grades and skipping school and after spending most of my life being the one who moved away, who changed twelve different schools before being in this high school, I'd never really experienced what it was like to be the one left behind.

> I surround myself in blankets and pillows and tiny things that have your scent—hoping that the night numbing my exhausted mind will play a trick and you will be beside me.

It's lines like this that remind me that other teens my age were busy getting drunk, going to parties, doing drugs, and having actual sex. They exhausted their minds with fun, instead of "flowing words."

The night before Super Mario Brothers Boy left, he carved out a little time to say goodbye to me.

We drove somewhere on that long, empty road where Nice Boy and I had our run-in with Officer Friendly. We parked on the side of the road and climbed into the backseat, the confessional booth of the small-town teenager.

I was distraught.

"I'm never going to see you again," I kept saying, not even bothering to hide my tears. "This is it. This is the last time we're ever going to see each other."

"Pam, that's not true."

"How could that not be true? You're moving to New York. I live in Texas."

"But life is long. And I know we're always going to know each other."

"There's no way that could possibly be true."

I'd moved almost every six months during grade school. I went to two different junior highs. The only person still in my life after all those moves was Holly Hunter Boy, and that had a lot to do with my own persistence. Super Mario Brothers Boy wasn't a phone talker and he was certainly no letter writer. I knew this was it. This was our real goodbye, and I couldn't believe he was refusing to say goodbye to me.

I wanted him to "say goodbye" to me. Like, in the Little Pam way. I needed this moment—my last time with him to be my first time with anyone. I don't remember if I had a boyfriend at the time or if he was sticking firmly to his rule that we were too good of friends to do anything that could potentially destroy our friendship. (This rule could be broken by sleep-kissing, but not much more.) I wanted him to take this goodbye seriously and hold me while I wept and maybe kissed a few tears away. I needed our *Say Anything*…moment in the backseat while Peter Gabriel played and we debated whether or not he was shaking.

I needed to see him sad, so that it didn't seem like I was the only one mourning the end of us.

"I'm going to always know you," he said again. "Look at me. Look me in the eyes. I am not kidding. This isn't over. We will always know each other. I can't imagine any other option."

It didn't sound romantic to me. It sounded like a bunch of bullshit. It sounded like things you say so you don't have to kiss a girl goodbye. He didn't even have to have sex with me. I'd settle for a hickey. I needed some kind of going-away present. Some kind of brain fodder so I wouldn't go home to write this:

> The ticking clock becomes your breath, it brushes on
> the back of my neck—I swear I feel it!—but it is only the
> fan swirling the lonely air of this too dark, too empty
> room. I am lost in its vastness.

I mean, somebody give this girl something to drink. Honestly. Super Mario Brothers Boy said his (chaste) goodbyes and left. I wrote letters. I made videotapes. I talked to him as if he had become an imaginary friend. He thought he'd see me again, but I knew there was just no way. He might as well have moved to Mars.

> I long for the quiet confines of our first paradise where
> we could be ourselves undiscovered until the morning.

But the blankets just don't cover me in the way that your arms can. I clutch the pillow tighter and tighter and try all I can but there isn't a heartbeat. No rise and fall. No gentle dream sighs. No comfort. No one to quiet my nightmares.

My cat comes to visit upon my chest to soothe my tears, but hears a noise in another room and continues his rounds.

That last part probably happened. Not the sleeping with the boy thing, just the cat part.

No constant calming. No gentle murmuring in my ear. No warmth.

My skin craves the feel of your flesh, just the toss of your leg over mine would pascify [sic] me. Your hair brushing against my arm as you turn in your sleep…

I am in agony.

I always assumed he'd come back to that town; that he'd just be there again some day. I was sure he'd find a way to drive his father crazy, that he would get himself in trouble enough that he'd be sent back.

I was upset he was gone, not just because we would never consummate our awkward romance, but because he was gone without me. We both wanted to escape that town; he was the only person I knew who hated it there more than I did. I lost one of the only people who would consistently turn to me and say, "You're not crazy; that's fucked up."

I was mad at him for being unable to keep his shit together, that we couldn't plan any kind of escape because he would never be on my time table. He would never want the things I wanted. He didn't even want to be in a relationship with me—how were we supposed to plan our future together?

"Absense [sic] makes the heart grow fonder..." and the body colder. I need the warmth of your embrace, your kiss, your touch—Just be in the same room as I and I could at least get some sleep, some rest, some remedy for my wandering soul and aching, aching heart.

Who's going to steal the sheets? Sleep on my pillow? Nudge me in my side so even in my dreams I know I'm not alone.

Not Super Mario Brothers Boy. Ever.

Because I am alone.

Without you, there is no inward peace. Something is missing as vital as a limb. A breath. A heartbeat. I cannot live!

I miss you miserably.

When I didn't hear from Super Mario Brothers Boy right away, I knew I was right—he was forever gone. There wasn't anything I could do, and that somehow only made it feel worse. I wanted to take to bed, like the days of yore, pale and corsetted, dying of an actual broken heart. I wanted to just give up. I wanted those things because the Internet hadn't been invented yet and my world was still very, very, suffocatingly small.

Let's steal each other and run away to our secret hideaway and hold each other for ransom. Let's lock each other in a room and swallow the key. In my mind, we already have.

Now if only I could just feel you...

Goodnight, my love. Sweet dreams and warm embraces.

Always...

ℓ

The envelope from Holly Hunter Boy arrives. It is thick, addressed in a handwriting I haven't seen in over twenty years. I can feel the notebook through the puffy packaging. After all this time, my note has come back to me.

I'm nervous to open it, anxious over how much will be proven apocryphal. These two hundred pages started the thousands upon thousands I've written since. This was my first book, my first essay, my first blog. Holly Hunter Boy was my first audience. Will flipping through these pages make me feel nostalgic, or will it remind me of the years I cried every day, wishing for a different life?

I leave the envelope on my desk, unopened.

7-3-92

I cannot kiss you. Your body lies next to me and I can feel the edge of your hand brush against mine—my nerves tingle. I want to know what you're thinking, what you're feeling.

I want to kiss you, but my strength and my courage tells me not to, so I don't. But I'm dying to know your feelings. Do they match mine?

I shouldn't kiss you. My heart has pledged eternal love to another. I do love him. But these feelings for you are something...different.

I will not kiss you, but instead ask what you are thinking. "Thinking about you," is your reply. What are you feeling? You look at me, take my hand and kiss it.

I need not another answer.

I would give you a picture of what I looked like right now at seventeen, but instead I will tell you that inserted in this page of my journal is a Gary Larson cartoon for "Cow Poetry," and a receipt for three boxes of incense and a rose quartz crystal.

7-14-92

"Don't step in that puddle," he tells her quietly. He'd hate to see her ruin her new shoes. She liked them so much when she got them. He's glad he saw the puddle before it was too late.

"I know," she says bitterly. "I don't need you nagging me all the time. Do this, do that. I swear, you're worse than my mother."

"Sorry," he mumbles, and turns his head down. He walks heel-toe, heel-toe, balancing on an imaginary wire on the highway. He keeps his thumb out just in case someone will stop for them because he knows she sometimes forgets their purpose (more to make sure that he doesn't say anything to her than to play a game). Better not to look at her at all; the temptation may be too great.

He staggers a little, and tries to regain his balance. He has one foot in a puddle, the other wobbles hovering above. His head is down and his arms flail up as he hears a screech and looks up too late to scream as she is hit by the car that was going to drive them home.

I Still Have All Your Marbles

...an answer...

I try

To tell you what I feel.

I can't help that there aren't words for it.

What do you call someone who falls in between your little brother and your lover?

You call him [*YOU KNOW I CAN'T TELL YOU HIS NAME AFTER THAT DESCRIPTION. POSSIBLY BECAUSE I THINK I COULD GO TO JAIL, MAYBE EVEN STILL AFTER ALL THESE YEARS.*]

Maybe you don't think the name is fitting.

But I do.

[*BOY I OWE ALL THE APOLOGIES TO*] is someone who you can trust, talk to, or laugh with.

Someone who always welcomes a hug

And will eagerly give one out

Someone who stays when you're hurting him (because he knows you don't realize it)

Someone who is persistant [sic] enough to remind you he's around (even when you don't need the reminder)

Someone who is probably too romantic for his own good (though no one seems to mind)

He expresses emotion without shame

Or fear

Or regret (well...maybe a little)

He knows what to say and when to say it.

He knows how to be adorable and a nasty little shit at the same time.

He knows when to walk away

And when to hold on with both hands.

I guess everyone has a [*JESUS, I'M SO SORRY TO THIS BOY IN PARTICULAR. REALLY, I CAN'T GO INTO IT HERE BECAUSE IF HE'S READING THIS ALL I NEED HIM TO KNOW IS THAT I'M SO SORRY FOR EVERYTHING I DID TO HIS HEART.*] in their lives. Someone who gives you an ego boost (even when you probably shouldn't have one) and someone who can break your heart with a look (which he's perfected, believe me).

I don't know if you understand or even believe what I've told you, if you believe in a [*BOY WHO I SOUL-CRUSHED ON A NEAR-DAILY BASIS*], if such a friend is possible.

You have a point: there will never be a [*I'M SORRY, YOU WERE IMPORTANT TO ME*] *better than* the [*I'M SO SORRY, I DIDN'T KNOW WHAT TO DO*].

Sure glad I found the right one.

[**FOREVER, SORRY. FOREVER.**]

Sometimes You Just Need
a Boy in a Crane Pose

…I would have done anything for another
hour to spend with each of them…

Stay

They ask her. She lies between them, they tighten their
grip on her. One clutches her embracing arm against
him, the other holds her tighter.

I have instant recollection of this night, this bed, these two
boys. I suppose you could think, at first, that I'm describing
something kinky or a little sexy, but then you should remember
that this is me we're talking about, so I'm describing something
where there's a lot of clothes being worn and there was just some
light cuddling. There are toddler music classes that see more
frottage than I was dishing out back then.

Stay

They repeat. She is weak, and waits another ten minutes,
feeling safety knowing she is loved.

Ten minutes ends.

Stay

They ask again. Their clutches again become together.
She loves them too much to say no.

She waits five minutes, then kisses their cheeks goodbye, and walks into the room of the one she adores and kisses him goodnight.

He reaches out for her, and her heart breaks a third time as she departs from her beloved, leaving his yearning hand outstretched.

She drives home

Alone. Sings to herself to keep herself company. She knows she is late, so she goes faster. The accelerator is on the floor.

This is true of the car I had in high school. You had to mash the accelerator or the brake to get them to do anything.

She runs a red light

But she doesn't care.

I used to do that, too. The red lights would last forever and there'd be nobody around for miles—you'd be at the top of this hill waiting for minutes with clearly nobody coming for a very long time and sometimes you've missed curfew because you've been stalling in the middle of a chaste threesome for like, fifteen minutes, and you've just got to floor it and say, "Fuck the red lights—I'M LIVING MY LIFE!"

Five more minutes they had asked again. Please, five more minutes. She had to say no. One more night, he had asked. Please, one more night. She had to say no.

She passes an ambulance and she wonders if there's someone in it—if there is, then if the person is living or dead or wishing to be dead or wishing for

Five more minutes or

One more night.

She didn't notice either the speed or the approaching car and she hit head on.

She should have stayed.

Did you think I was finally going to end a story without the death of the main character? I thought so, too! But no. Death. It comes after almost-threesomes, every time.

I was spending a lot of time with these two boys, one of whom was Apology Boy from the last letter; the other was Nice Boy's brother. There was a time when the three of us were inseparable.

The nature of honors classes meant that you pretty much spent your entire school day with the same thirty kids moving from classroom to classroom. Extra-curriculars aside, there were very few options to take you away from the students that were going to take every test sitting next to you for four years and until we all graduate in the top thirty places in our class.

Our valedictorian-to-be was a unique, sometimes manipulative, often infuriating boy. He was intelligent and inquisitive. Impish. Tall, with a mop of messy curls, he had a few physical tics—he'd sniff, rub the tip of his nose with his fingers, fidget. Nothing on him ever stayed still, from his mouth to his body. And he was funny. Quick-witted, with an eye for the absurd. He was very smart and came from a big family. His father was well-respected in the religious community. I was close with his older brother.

Smart Boy and I had a lot of classes together. Which means we spent a lot of time together. Then when his best friend started hanging around my ex-boyfriend Nice Boy all the time, we found ourselves together even more than usual, which led to us darting around that space where you figure out if maybe you're going to get involved with each other.

Ultimately we didn't. And he didn't like that.

From that point on, it appeared one of his hobbies was pissing me off. It was deliberate, daily, and designed to hurt my feelings. The attacks were unpredictable and sometimes childish. He placed a personal ad in the school paper that called me a tease who ate through blonde boys like candy. He used the lyrics to "I Wanna Sex You Up." I cannot hear that song without my stomach dropping in memory. Other times his vitriol was viciously inappropriate. In Academic Decathlon class one day, he suggested to a classmate who was having a disagreement with me about an assignment, "Just make fun of her for being molested. It shuts her up every time."

That classmate, so thrown off by the statement, stood up and walked right out of the room. "Why would you say that?" he asked as he left. It was a question people often asked Smart Boy, who would just shrug and smile. "People say all kinds of things," he'd sometimes respond. He liked statements that were true, but usually left unspoken. He questioned everything. He would find amusement in others' frustration. And I think he wanted an apology from me, one where I confessed to some sort of manipulation on my part. He believed I had wanted him to fall for me, only so I could reject him.

It came to a head one night when a few of us were hanging out in the bedroom of Nice Boy's Brother. Apology Boy, the brother, and I were all on the bed, goofing off with the ceiling fan light switch, which was dangling overhead. (See: the description of our earlier threesome.) Smart Boy and another friend of ours were in the room, too. We were listening to music, talking about school, just bullshitting around before we all had to leave, when Apology Boy flicked the light off again—

—and Smart Boy attacked.

It was fast and it was disorienting. Who was on top of us? Why was there someone punching us? How were we being hit? As soon as I realized Smart Boy was on us, and it was his fists I was feeling, I immediately pulled Nice Boy's Brother under me. He had epilepsy and a blow to the head could cause a seizure. Apology Boy was struggling to turn the light back on and finally he did.

The light was on and we were still. I'm on the bed, Nice Boy's Brother behind me. Apology Boy is on the floor, looking up at Smart Boy, who is standing with his fists balled, panting.

Off to the side, our other friend is standing with his hair wild, mouth open, panting. He's in the crane pose from *The Karate Kid*.

While that in and of itself was funny, the only sound in the room was the CD playing, which was *Infectious Grooves'* "Closed Session." You probably don't know the skit, but all you need to know is there's a man singing, "*Whipped Cream! Put it all over your BODY!*"

To keep the solemnity of the moment, Apology Boy quietly reached up and pressed the "off" button.

When Smart Boy finally spoke, he said he had to do what he'd done because he was the only person who truly loved me and who would ever truly love me. "I realize you won't speak to me again, but I had to do it because I had to wake you up. I had to wake all of you up. Your parents don't love you. These people don't love you. All these boys, they don't love you. You just don't get it."

The other boys began trying to calm him down, trying to get him out of the room, away from me, because it was clear he might spring again, that he wasn't finished with all he had to say, and he was still very angry. This was when Nice Boy's Mom got involved, asking what was going on, who was doing all that yelling.

I was sequestered, and I heard Karate Kid Boy start to pull Smart Boy away from the house. "I'm driving you home," I heard him say.

"DAMMIT! YOU'RE ALL GOING TO TAKE HER AWAY!"

That's the last thing I heard Smart Boy say before he was out of the house.

Nice Boy's Mom, one of my favorite moms of all time, pulled me into a hug. "Okay, so you can stay here, as long as you want."

"I think I should go home," I said. I felt too exposed, too confused. I didn't often choose my home as the safe place, but I knew the longer I stayed there, the more I was giving Smart Boy the chance to find me later on my drive home. I just wanted to go home and be hugged by someone safe.

Nice Boy's Mom called Smart Boy's parents to tell them what happened. His father asked to speak with me.

He asked me not to tell anybody about what had happened. "Especially at school. We just don't want to hurt his chances at college. He's got such a bright future."

This was what all the parents kept saying. Nice Boy's Mom and Apology Boy's parents felt the same way. "Why make trouble for him?"

It wasn't that I wanted to tell everybody what had happened, but as I stared at the bruise that had formed on my arm, I thought, *Why is he the one everybody's worrying about protecting?*

"I'm terribly sorry about this," Smart Boy's Dad said to me on that phone call. "Is there anything I can do?"

"You can get your son some help."

Nice Boy's Mom suggested I take an alternate route on my drive home. She was wise. The next day Karate Kid Boy told me that Smart Boy had made him park right off a dark corner I had to turn down to get to my subdivision. He made him wait there for an hour.

My parents had been briefed on what had happened from Nice Boy's Mom, but once I got home they wanted to hear it from me.

"This is what happens when you spend so much time with these boys," Dad said. "They get confused. They get too involved. You make these relationships that are too intense, too unrealistic, no wonder he snapped, no wonder he thought he could do that to you."

"THIS IS NOT MY FAULT!"

I don't know where the words came from, or how I found the strength to shout them, but I was yelling in my living room, yelling until my throat hurt and my eyes burned. It was so late and I was so tired and I couldn't believe that when I finally chose to come home to the safety of my parents, I was told that what had just happened was all on me.

"I didn't make anyone hit me! There's nothing I could have done that would make it okay for someone to hit me. Why don't you believe that, too? He's the one who hit me. He's the one who did something wrong. He's not the one we're all supposed to be so worried about! You're my parents and you're supposed to be on my side!"

This happened just before a lock-in at the school for our theatre production, which we were both in. (Do they still do lock-ins at high schools, or have they finally figured out that's how babies get made?)

During the lock-in I did my best to avoid Smart Boy, but when I walked into what I thought was an empty dressing room, he was there, staring at himself in a mirror. When I turned to leave, he grabbed my wrist.

"What's that?" he said, pointing at the bruise on my arm.

"That's from you," I said. "You know that."

"No. I never hit you. I didn't hit you."

"You did."

"No. I was careful. I made sure I never hit you. It wasn't you I was trying to hit."

"You hit me. This is from you."

He began to shake, muttering to himself, "No, no, no," over and over, and I left. Behind me, I could hear him yelling at himself, presumably staring into the mirror again, becoming even more terrifying to me.

Smart Boy sat beside me in every class. My calculus teacher—a man who prided himself on his reputation for being strict but was one of those curmudgeons who was secretly super softy on the inside once you got to know him—was walking the aisles during a test when he stopped at my desk. He pointed at my arm, his finger near the dark-purple bruise.

"What is that?" he asked.

"Nothing," I answered.

"Stay after class."

That remains the only time I was ever asked to stay after class to discuss a problem.

Once everybody left, my teacher asked what happened.

"Jesus, Pam. Why is your life so *Sleeping with the Enemy*?"

"I know. I'm sorry."

"It's not your fault. But why didn't I hear about this already?"

"Because they told us not to tell anybody."

My calculus teacher grunted as he crossed his arms, thinking. "Well, don't worry about him," he said. "I'll take care of it."

Things changed after that. My calculus teacher went out of his way to harass Smart Boy every day in class, including one time walking all the way from the outside parking lot to Smart Boy's desk to blow a mouthful of cigarette smoke in his face. I have no idea how long he had to hold his breath to do that, and my calculus teacher was a hardcore smoker, so he must have been determined.

It wasn't just my calculus teacher who had changed. Word must have spread, because the attitudes toward Smart Boy were definitely different, sometimes in a delightfully subversive way. In English class, my friend and I had to recite "The Walrus and the Carpenter." Smart Boy sat in the front row of that class, twelve inches from where I was standing.

"*The sea was wet as wet can be...*"

We tossed a bucket of water on Smart Boy. The class erupted in laughter, applause. Two months earlier I would've been too scared to try a joke like that in a classroom, especially at his expense. Now it was applauded like everyone wanted to see me get some kind of revenge. Unspoken encouragement. Our English teacher just gave a quiet nod of approval.

"*The sands were dry as dry.*"

We tossed a cup of flour on his face.

A couple of weeks later, I find a twenty-page letter on my car. It outlines, in detail, everything he thought was wrong with me and everything I'd done to make him do what he did. I don't remember much of it, but I do remember thinking, *Maybe from now on I should keep my notes to boys a little more on the short side.*

When I look back on the night Smart Boy attacked us, remembering how sad and confused I was when I went to bed, having yelled at my father for the first time in my life, I feel a dark heaviness inside.

That was the first time I tried to figure out if I was supposed to change my behavior, be a different person than I was, in order to keep men from doing things I would never think to do to someone else. It wouldn't be the only time in my life someone suggested I'd done something to invite violence upon me or asked if I "deserved" the treatment I was getting. Back when the boys had broken into the house to steal my money and my videotapes, I took some responsibility, even though I hadn't done anything to warrant a break-in and a threat. I took the responsibility so that I could understand it, so that I could convince myself that I could control something like that from happening again. If I changed my own behavior, maybe I could prevent further violence, further attacks.

Part of the reason I spent years not wanting to have children was because I was afraid of having a daughter who could one day be forced to claim responsibility for something that never should have happened to her.

We're asked what we did to bring upon us these acts of selfish rage. We're asked why we didn't fight harder, didn't shout louder, didn't love better. We're asked questions that have no answer, because they don't deserve one.

One afternoon, just before graduation, my father appeared at my bedroom door. "There's someone here to see you."

Smart Boy was sitting at our dining room table. "My parents are having me apologize to everyone," he said.

"Okay, bye."

I hurried back to the safety of my bedroom, terror-tears filling my eyes, only stopping to ask my father, "How could you let him in this house? How much do you hate me?"

Years later, after my father had died, my mother told me what happened after I'd slammed my bedroom door.

Dad walked Smart Boy out to the driveway. And then he said, "I only let you in because she deserved an apology from you. Now you stay the hell away from my daughter for the rest of her life, or I will kill you."

This is What I Wrote in My Journal on My Eighteenth Birthday.

…written in Calculus…

Scattered thoughts. Mumbled thoughts. A bird trips over its wing and falls through the air to its death. Funny how gravity helps until it hurts. Funny. A small girl sits on her bed tying her shoes. Attempt number three-hundred. Success? She unties her fingers out of the knot but she can't because they are stuck, her fingers turning the color of her purple, purple laces. She whimpers, cries, "Someone help me!" She calls for Mommy. Shouts, tears roll down her face and hit her bounded pointer fingers. Will she still be able to play the game if she loses them? Where is pointer, where is pointer? Gone, gone, gone. Lost in a shoelace accident. She gets scared. She'll never be able to turn five if she doesn't have enough fingers to show for it. Mommy, mommy, mommy she screams. Will she be helped? Will someone notice her? In the next room Mommy sits with tears dripping onto her own instrument of bondage. The moisture makes it sparkle, the gold and diamond catches a glare in the tears dripping from her eyelashes. She's been struggling for seven years to free herself. Attempt number three-thousand. Success? She rocks back and forth, sitting on her feet, pulling on her heart and fears. She isn't strong enough. She isn't strong enough. She's trying and she's crying and she's trying and she's scared and she's trying and she hears her baby's screams in the next room. If only she could hold her but she's bound to her place. If only they could find each other, help each other, face each other's fears.

I Get Tongue-Tied

In all the millions of words in the world, why is it so impossible to describe emotions as vividly as tears do?

I am eighteen. I live with my parents. I am no longer in high school but I haven't yet started college and I was feeling a lot of things.

Things like—it was important to me that I didn't go to college with a boyfriend. This was difficult to explain to certain people, namely my boyfriend, Apology Boy. He wanted to hang on just a few months longer, until they maybe stretched into a year or two or three or all and then one day he would no longer be in high school either, and then we could get married.

I lived in Texas, where this was considered the ultimate love story.

But I had big plans and big dreams and I knew it was important that I get to college completely unattached for I was a virgin and this meant all of my new first times were to be filled with college importance. Independence! I was my own woman! Perhaps I would go on birth control!

So I broke up with my boyfriend, which sent a very confusing message to this other boy I knew who would sometimes visit my bedroom window late at night. At the time I just thought we had a very *Romeo and Juliet* thing going on. Although Romeo and Juliet had sex, so I don't know what I thought was happening. *"I guess he just likes hanging out with me in the middle of the night! We are such good friends. They should make a movie about us!"*

Actually, you can tell exactly what I thought was going on if you return to my diary from that night, where I'd written the following short story.

> He came to her in the middle of the night (he must have walked five miles, at least). Braving the biting winds at three am. He crawled into her bedroom window, careful not to kick the glowing candle on her windowsill. Did she know he was coming? She couldn't possibly.

She did. That was our code I'd leave him that meant it was safe for him to come over—my parents were in bed or not home or whatever. Don't judge the lack of parental supervision. I'm eighteen—I'M AN ADULT. I MAKE ADULT CHOICES LIKE WHICH CANDLE SHOULD I LIGHT ON THE WINDOWSILL TONIGHT THAT IS WELCOMING BUT NOT TOO SKANKY?

> The candle brought a faint smell of strawberry into the small room. He stepped inside and closed the window behind him. He found her lying on her bed—asleep. She wore a gown of white, which had caught on her thighs as she tossed in her sleep. One hand was tucked under her turned chin; the other was wrapped around her middle. Her hair made an angelic halo about her face, the candle catching it, making her appear even more heavenly.

Indeed.

> He sat down beside her, his only light the candle. The sight of her melted any traces of cold on him. He stared at her for a few minutes and then looked up. It surprised him, at first, that when he caught his face in the mirror he was smiling.

What I love about that is how much I just think I'm awesome.

> He leaned down to her and kissed her lightly on the forehead. She made no stir. He grabbed her hand and as

she awoke he placed his other hand over her mouth. She widened her eyes, then relaxed. They widened again.

Specificity in softcore porn is important, you guys.

"What are you doing here?" she asked.

"I had to see you," he whispered.

"Why?" Her brow furrowed.

He looked at her and a smile came across his face. He broke his stare to flip back his hair and then looked again as he leaned down to give his reply in a kiss.

Just a kiss, because saying, "I was hoping after I walked five miles in the icy cold and then Jack-Be-Nimbled into your strawberry-scented room, you'd give me a blowjob" might make you not give me a blowjob.

She reached up and pulled him towards her. He kicked off his shoes and crawled into the bed with her. They kissed each other—the ultimate silent conversation—until she heard him give a small sigh.

—of disappointment.

She looked at him with a smile.

"What?" she whispered.

He paused, stared at her, and said, "You."

"Me? What about me?" She kissed his neck, his ear, his cheek, his lips.

"I love you."

She felt a rush undescribable [*sic*]. She kissed him over and over. Each kiss became more and more passionate until the only thing that existed was the feeling of their skin touching. They took off their clothes and sat, holding each other, her in his lap, legs wrapped around him with a dark blanket circling them both in warmth. They needed the feeling of flesh on flesh more than they needed anything else.

If there were a quiz—written or oral—I'm not sure "they" would both give that same answer.

They sat there, kissing and holding and talking until they got tired, where they laid down (her head on his bare chest, fingers tracing the definition of his stomach) and they talked until they fell asleep.

You guys. Think about it. If that happened to you tonight you'd be really happy. You'd probably talk until you fell asleep two or three times in one night if you could.

In the morning when she woke, she was clutching a pillow. Beside her bed lay a letter, reading:

I love you. Thank you.

On her windowsill her candle had become a puddle of dried wax. The curtains swayed back and forth in the breeze created by the open window.

(So at least that candle got fucked real good.)

And then there are three—THREE!—poems in a row about people trying to hold each other but falling asleep instead.

Many months went by. College was quickly approaching and I was getting more and more nervous. Would I really go to college a virgin? Maybe I needed experience. And there was this boy who would climb through my bedroom window in the middle of the night. And it was clear that he was very interested in taking off his clothes and having me sit in his lap with a blanket wrapped around us while candles burned. I mean, actually, he was. He was very "My mom made us costumes to wear to the Ren Faire" and wrote poems that repeatedly used the phrase "in my mind's eye" — but he also would probably want to do more than just kiss and hold until we fell asleep.

So one night he came in through the bedroom window and stumbled onto my daybed and no doubt the song playing on my little personal stereo was "Summertime Rolls" by Jane's Addiction. He climbed into my room and maybe I'm wearing something white, and I'm waiting for this boy to arrive, and I am rehearsing how I'm going to tell him that tonight we can maybe do a little more than just hold each other but maybe it's better if I don't tell him and I just show him or let him lead, I should let him lead, right? He's running late and I'm getting a little tired, but I'm sure he's on his way. Did I just fall asleep? Oh, he's here. He's here.

He's here and I'm quietly in bed and I can't turn any of the lights on because I am in my parents' house and they definitely do not want any boy in their house in the middle of the night so he climbs in and then I hear something so he

RUNS TO THE CLOSET. HURRY HURRY SHHHHHHH OH GOD OH OH GOD OH GOD

He's in the closet and I'm by my bedroom door listening and it's really all quite magical and romantic because he doesn't know but I know tonight there will be bases rounded and I think whatever I heard was maybe just the pipes or my cat or something so it's okay, he can come out but it's hard to see in just that candlelight so he trips on my diary which was on the floor and that DEFINITELY made someone hear something so he's back in the closet and I'm in my bed pretending to be asleep and my father opens the door and says WHAT THE HELL IS THAT CANDLE DOING LIT? YOU TRYING TO BURN THIS HOUSE DOWN? And holy shit that was close but now he's gone and maybe he could come out of the closet QUIETLY and probably maybe crawl this time because SHHH and okay, now he can't look at himself in the mirror and catch his smile, but he's probably still pretty happy to see me. Or not see me, since it's so dark, but he's still—this is still. This IS ALL GOING FINE, YOU GUYS.

So he crawls into my bed and it makes a squeak so we sit very still for a really long time and I'm starting to get tired but he's kissing me so I kiss back and it's very *our flesh is melding* or whatever I said earlier; it's still romantic.

So I say, "You can do more tonight. I want an experience."

Where is he going? Oh, he's going under the covers I...oh, he's going down to my—oh, okay, that's I guess going to happen but I... Okay, that's...okay, this is very college life. I should probably get used to this happening to me...in the dark...um.

Bffffthhh. Am I supposed to close my eyes or keep them open? Should I be thinking so much? I probably shouldn't be thinking so much. But...it's...what he's doing is...That can't be...That's just an old Sam Kinison routine, he can't have taken that as knowledge or advice, right? No, that's...I'm definitely sensing a pattern here. Don't ask him don't ask him don't ask him—

"Are you licking the alphabet?

...I said, 'Are you licking the alphabet?'

...I can tell.

...I said, 'I can tell!' Shh!"

SHHH!...............

"Okay, I think I didn't hear anything. Sorry."

I shouldn't have bothered him. Okay, no thinking. No counting. Those aren't letters anymore, they're just...swirls. Swirls and...a little nothing. Now nothing. Hmm. That's weird. I'm tired and nothing's happening.

Ow. Was I just asleep? OW! Okay, something hurts. Ow!

"I'm sorry. I don't mean to bother you. But...you're kind of hurting me and I don't understand why. Could you maybe leave that area?

"...What? You what? Come? You got CUM on me?? Oh, GUM? Wait, you got gum on me?! Where? Why did you have gum in your mouth? No, I didn't know that! Why would I know that?"

And I move my hand down there and you guys, I'm just a tangle of pubic hair and Doublemint. It is a remarkable mess.

"Get out of here! Just go! Because you got gum in my pubes, that's why! I have to take care of this! I don't know—peanut butter? Just get out, get out! Asshole! God!"

And he stumbles back through the window into the sticky summer night air. I tiptoe to the kitchen for peanut butter and ice and ultimately my razor, and that's why I'm taking a shower at 3:00 A.M. shaving off all my pubes, my virginity safely intact.

In the morning, I take to my diary, where everything is better. Where everything is safe and lovely and clean. I write the following:

A hot night.
Lovers entwined.
Our mouths wanting, full of surprises.
My bed waits for you.
A night to remember.
You tangled me up in your love.

I Swear I Recognize Your Breath

Why do we measure our love in time?
Two months four months six months eight months
Why not measure it in intensity?
Our only marker
The passionate kiss, the lingering looks, the sparkle in
our fixed eyes.
Is it because there isn't a figure high enough to capture
its true intensity?
I thought so.

About a month into my freshman year of college, I am visited
by GumPubes Boy. He has travelled exactly 142 miles to see me,
the distance from my old town to my new home of Austin, Texas.

We hug in the parking lot of my dormitory. "Happy one-
month anniversary," he says.

Oh, shit, what? Happy whaaaaaa? I am frozen, wide eyes and a
pursed mouth, as I mulled over the exploits of my past few weeks.

There was the party I went to where I thought I was seeing
crack being smoked, but it turned out to just be a bong, and I had
my first experience with pot that ended with me kissing a guy I'd
just met for about fifteen minutes before we both got hungry and
then fell asleep.

There was the double date with the grad students at a Japanese
indie film that was kind of just porn, where the girl in the other
couple was clearly interested in my date and spent a lot of time

making fun of how young I was. That night ended with me at my date's apartment, climbing the ladder to his loft bed—officially the coolest thing you could ever even conceive of when you are eighteen—and learning that sometimes when you tell a boy you're a virgin, he responds to that by getting as far away from your mouth as possible, opting to suck on your toes for about half an hour before you fall asleep.

I don't know what it was about my body parts getting lots of attention, but there was another night where a boy I'd been hanging out with just started randomly making out with my hand. Like, really going to town, finger by finger. What base is that? Because that's the only one we rounded that night. I can't think about it for too long or I start to remember how wet the space between my fingers got that night, and how I was sitting on a bed, watching a boy attack my fingers like they were made of Popsicles.

So when GumPubes said, "Happy one-month anniversary!" I didn't know what else to say other than, "You too!" I spent the rest of our weekend together trying to determine what exactly happened on the day he considered us to have officially gotten together, hoping it didn't coincide with that Doublemint fiasco.

GumPubes lived far away, and with *even more apologies* to Apology Boy, I decided it wasn't the worst thing in the world to have a boyfriend back home while I was at college. GumPubes went about the process of transferring to my school while I focused more on schoolwork and less on getting my appendages sucked.

"I'll write to you," he promised.

And he did. Oh, how he did. With the intensity and passion that Little Pam had always hoped she'd find. Every day, another letter in the mail, sometimes two. And I wrote back just as often. Pages and pages of letters to each other about our lives, our hopes, our dreams, our plans. We talked flowers and sunsets and movies and poetry. Art and childhoods and inappropriate jokes. He painted. He drew. If you squinted, he looked a little like Kurt Cobain. Who could ask for anything more?

Things were going just fine until the beginning of November, when I got a phone call from Super Mario Brothers Boy. "I'm coming to town," he said. "I have a bus ticket, and I'm coming in for Thanksgiving weekend. If it's okay, I'd like to stay with you and then ride with you back home for the holiday."

GumPubes was a very sensitive-ponytail-boy kind of boy. I mentioned earlier how he used phrases like "in my mind's eye," but it still doesn't explain why I felt I had any right to do what I did next.

I stood in that same parking lot where he had declared our one-month anniversary, and I calmly, rationally explained how Super Mario Brothers Boy was coming to town in a couple of weeks, and I was going to lose my virginity to him.

I told him about our history, how he was keeping a promise that he'd see me again, how I never thought I'd have this second chance to be with him, that this was the end of our love story, that this was our promise to each other.

"And you discussed this?" he asked. "You two have planned for this to happen?"

"Well, no," I said. "He asked to stay with me. It would be weird if we talked about it. It's just what's expected. This is like a promise we made."

And I don't know, I guess sensitive ponytail boys are suckers for romance, because GumPubes was like, "Okay. I can't stand in the way of this."

You guys; we didn't break up. He was just all, "See you after Thanksgiving."

He must have thought I'd come to my senses, that I'd realize I was asking the impossible here, and eventually I'd come running through the rain to his door, begging him to forgive me, banging on his windows, yelling, "I didn't do it! I couldn't do it! I just kept thinking of you!"

Super Mario Brothers Boy's bus arrived on a Tuesday afternoon. I picked him up at the station. I hadn't seen him in almost two years and he'd grown taller, thinner. He'd still kept his boyish appearance, but had been working hard to cover it with facial hair, tattoos. We hugged. He smelled awful.

"I need a shower," he said. "I've been on that thing for days."

My plan went immediately into action. Super Mario Brothers Boy didn't know it, but my entire dorm wing was dancing with excitement over Operation Virginity Loss. My roommate had already made plans to sleep in another room. The girl with the handicapped shower in her suite had offered to let Super Mario Brothers Boy bathe in her room, as the rest of our girls' dorm only had communal showers. We'd orchestrated the entire night around the dorm's enforced 9:00 P.M. curfew. I was to take SMB Boy out for dinner and a sunset, and I'd get him into my dorm by 8:45 P.M., "forgetting" to sign him in. Girls on the other end of the hall were going to have a loud-ish party, so that any RA's who passed by would be more concerned about the noise they were making instead of what might be going on in my room.

Because I don't want to undersell it, you have to understand that my freshman year dorm hall was filled with the nicest, sweetest girls I've ever met. They were chipper and cheery, very peppy and nerdy. We had a Southern sorority girl, a positively gleeful Buddhist, a long-skirted Pentacostal, a free-love touting Japanese-German model, a spunky cheerleader, a sensitive artist, and a girl so sheltered I had to teach her what a tampon was. And every single one of them was stoked to participate in The Night Pam Loses Her Virginity To Her High School Love.

After Super Mario Brothers Boy took a shower in the wheelchair-access room, he was going through his duffel bag in the corner of my room. "Hey, have you heard from [Soft Hair]? He lives here."

I had learned that a month earlier, when a dancer in the show I was stage managing, the prettiest girl I'd ever seen in my life, casually dropped her boyfriend's name when she heard where I'd gone to high school. At first I thought perhaps she was mistaken. He had a common enough name, and a tendency to kiss boys, so she probably had something mixed up.

But then she described his hair. And my heart broke in a spectacularly new and confusing way. Was this how pretty I had to be in order to make a guy be not gay? Because I was never going to be able to do it! She had dancer collarbones and model wrists. I had hips that would one day be an asset in roller derby.

I didn't say all of this to Super Mario Brothers Boy. I played it cool. "I haven't spoken to him, no. He's dating some girl, whatever."

"It'd be fun to see him, don't you think?"

"We'd better get to dinner."

"It's five in the afternoon."

But we had to eat then so we could get to Mount Bonnell before sunset. Mount Bonnell is a pretty viewing point that overlooks Lake Travis and is a popular spot for either Parents' Weekend, or making out with your high school soul mate.

It was also rather dangerous once it turned dark, because it lacked fences or railings. SMB Boy and I were walking to a more private location when I tripped and almost tumbled over the cliff's edge. It was such a close call even SMB Boy was alarmed.

"That would've sucked," he said.

"Yeah," I said. "I could've died."

"I meant you have the keys."

We made out as the sun went down and it was everything I'd hoped it would be, even though I couldn't get truly comfortable because we were on dust and rocks and I was constantly checking my watch. I had to get us back to the dorm. I didn't want us to be homeless and in my car for the night. In retrospect, that would've been pretty romantic.

Super Mario Brothers Boy wasn't too keen on the dorm. "Where am I going to pee?"

"In my sink. I'll leave the room."

"No, no. It's better if you look. See the real me."

"Ha."

"If you had fallen off that cliff, how would I get my stuff back from your room? My bus ticket is in there."

I got us back in the dorm well before 8:45, terrified that it would be hard to sneak him past the front desk if I waited any longer.

I put on some Pearl Jam, as that was the custom at the time.

Super Mario Brothers Boy asked to make a phone call, and I went down the hallway to where all my friends were waiting.

"How's it going?" they asked, faces full of smiles.

"Very well, thank you," I said. "Thanks again for helping."

"No problem. He's so cute. You guys are so cute together."

I went back to my room to find Super Mario Brothers Boy beaming. He kissed me and said, "I have a question for you."

"Okay."

"How about we go to [Soft Hair's] place?"

"What?"

"I just got off the phone with him and he's stoked to see me. Us. Both of us, you're invited, too. Come on, it'll be fun."

"But if we go there, we can't be here. I can't get you back in here."

"I can stay at his place, that's no big deal. You could stay, too. We could share a couch or something. The floor."

I was *not* going to lose my virginity on the floor of Soft Hair's apartment while he and his pretty girlfriend had sex on a proper bed. I mean, honestly, did this mean Soft Hair made me watch him kiss a boy just so he could break up with me? That's so *weird*.

"I don't want to go to his place," I said, not even bothering to hide my pout.

"Well, he's on his way to pick me up, so I'm going to go outside before you get in trouble for having me past curfew. You sure you don't want to come?"

"No! I can't believe you're leaving!"

"Come with me."

"No! Stay here. You said you wanted to stay here, with me."

"I don't want to pee in a sink and I don't want to get you in trouble."

"Fine. Just walk yourself out, just go, just get out of here, go away, forget it, just go."

I have this image forever burned in my head, and it's me standing in that dorm room, staring at the open door, and behind me I hear Eddie Vedder warbling through the speakers:

i just want to scream...hello...
my God its been so long, never dreamed you'd return
but now here you are, and here i am

And then all these heads pop in at the edges of the doorframe.

hearts and thoughts they fade...away...
hearts and thoughts they fade...away...

One friend after another, faces filled with concern. I'm standing there crying because hearts and thoughts they fade, fade away and girls are just streaming into my room, arms outstretched, all murmuring, *I can't believe he left* and *what a jerk* and *we love you so much* and *it's okay, I'll make some popcorn* and *at least you still have a boyfriend.*

Which I did. I still had a boyfriend. SMB Boy resurfaced two days later when he needed a ride back to our town for Thanksgiving. I drove him, of course. And when he asked about my new car, "How fast does this thing go?" I ended up getting my one and only speeding ticket.

In the end I lost my virginity the old-fashioned way—with my boyfriend, over Christmas break, while my parents were home discussing whether or not they wanted to get a divorce. I wanted to be away from home, I wanted to stop feeling pressured from my boyfriend to just get it over with, I wanted to feel that same weary-faced feeling my friend back at school would give me when she talked about her sex life. *"You'll understand some day, Pam,"* she'd say. *"When you're experienced."*

So, I went and got myself experienced. And it wasn't life-changing, it wasn't mind-blowing, it wasn't the start of a new chapter in my life. It didn't answer anything, it didn't heighten anything, and it certainly didn't change my perception of what love means, or what it could be. I was a virgin, and then I wasn't. After all of that searching, the answer was one I could never have imagined—losing your virginity gives you a memory of losing your virginity. That is it. You get that memory, and like all our life-long memories, it's important to choose it wisely. I made the active decision to wrap this memory up with my emotional turmoil at home. I couldn't have known that was about to happen even an hour earlier than it did, but once I decided, it felt like I'd always known it was going to happen. If my parents were going their separate ways, then it was time for me to grow up, too.

When I got home I saw a pair of wedding bands on the coffee table. That night everybody lost something. Everybody made a huge decision.

But in the morning, my parents put their rings back on, where they stayed for the rest of my father's life. My boyfriend and I broke up the following summer.

Holly Hunter Boy Speaks

P—

In some way, I feel that this needs some sort of disclaimer. I mean we're talking about liking people. I *like*-like my wife. Sure I had a life before I met her in junior high, but somehow I feel funny—not that she does, by the way. And also, you're asking me to think like a junior high boy. Thirteen-year-old boy reasoning doesn't always make sense—not that that is too different than now.

I can't believe you don't remember the Metallica fight!!! It was a big deal (if I remember correctly). But I did buy a new Swatch phone so I guess it turned out alright. And I agree but I'm not really a Black album kind of guy. I did like...*And Justice for All*, but over all, I think that the Cliff years were the best. But I'm excited about *Trujillo*.

[Our song was "Patience" by Guns N' Roses. Holly Hunter Boy doesn't know that. And that is because I never told him. —p]

What is your earliest memory of me? Meaning, how and when did you first notice me?

I honestly can't remember. But it is nothing personal, I can't remember what I did for dinner last night.

How would you have defined our relationship in the sixth grade?

I don't really remember anything from 6th grade except that time one of Mrs. J---s nephews visited ([She was] formerly Ms. Rice). And we all thought it might be Jerry Rice. It wasn't.

At a certain point you had to know I "liked you" liked you. Did it hit you at once, dawn on you, or was it clear because I told you?

Now we move on to 7th grade and [our junior high]. Remember, at the time, 6th grade wasn't considered jr. high. Now, [that school] houses 6th-8th grades or middle school- not 7-9th jr high. Kids these days.

I'm sure someone had to tell me. I'm not that observant when it comes to the ladies.

What did you think when you started getting all these notes from me?

I remember getting them and feeling special (but I also remember kinda expecting).

Did you ever think of trying to let me down gently?

Why would I do that? I got notes from you…but I seriously am not sure about why I'd let you down? You were my friend and I didn't want to lose that.

I seem to remember you always having a girlfriend (Allison, Carrie, Kelleyeyeeye).

[*Her name was spelled "Kellye" because of the South.*]

Was there ever a time you decided to keep a girlfriend around just a little longer than you wanted just to make sure you weren't available, or is it possible I am giving myself way too much real estate in your mind/heart that I never actually possessed?

A. I never dated Carrie.

B. I never put that much thought into it.

C. You probably had more real estate than you or I knew at the time. I mean, I had never actually seen Kelleyeye in real life at the time (did you know we ended up at the same high school and graduating together?)

[*I had NO IDEA they had never met in real life and were dating. I wasted a LOT of nights imagining them making out.*]

Do you remember watching *Broadcast News* with me?

I think you are making this up or confusing me with R----- C----l. I remember watching *1969* in [small town], TX with you.

[*I assure you I am not making that up. I do remember watching 1969 as well. It is funny to me that he mentions RC, as that was the first boy to ever tongue-kiss me. He was never my boyfriend, though.*]

Remember chauffeuring me on a date?

[*At first I thought I had blocked out a very important memory, but he's teasing me here. That is the history of us. I think he's being serious, I get frantic, then I realize he's kind of making fun of me for thinking I'm Mary Stuart Masterson in* Some Kind of Wonderful. *Every time. I fall for it every time.*]

I finally open the envelope.

The notebook slides out. It is 200 pages long. A green cover, just as I remembered. I've decorated it in peace signs and scrawled across the middle: "Merry Christmas, [Holly Hunter Boy]!" My handwriting is large and loopy and reminds me a lot of my younger sister's. I am disappointed to see it's the only thing inside the envelope. He didn't write a note. Some things never change.

11-30-88

[Holly Hunter Boy]-

Picture it. A note to beat all notes. The longest note you can think of. This is my Christmas present to you.

[*later, at the bottom of the page*]

Well, it's getting to the bottom of the page & I have to make a decision. Am I going to write on both sides?

[*page two*]

No. If I happen to write more than 200 pages, I'll buy another notebook. I bet you're wondering why I decided a note for your present. Well, you told me what you like to do. Play the Bass, Watch TV, play football, and eat. But you also like to get <u>notes</u>!

I go on to describe what my parents are watching on television, what I'm watching on television, what my friends are doing at that moment, who's on the phone with whom, and how many pages I've written so far.

[*page thirty-two*]

I just made myself Hot Chocolate. That's my favorite thing about the winter. Pouring my heart out and drinking hot chocolate.

On page thirty-four I recount an epic girl-fight that rearranged the social structure of my closest friends. I am clearly hurt to have been excluded and worrying that one of these girls, Carrie, will "take [Holly Hunter Boy] away from me." (This is the girl mentioned above whom I remember Holly Hunter Boy dating, but apparently I'm mistaken.) (I'm not sure I'm mistaken.) (I mean, look: we've learned time and again through this book that people don't have to know they're dating someone to be in a relationship.)

The pages are a tight time capsule of my life at thirteen. There are tiny notes included from my best friends, my sister. In some places I have taped comic strips I clipped from the newspaper (including one about a girl "pouring her heart out" in a note

she's writing in class, only to have it get taken up by the teacher—
meta!). I am testing out early jokes, establishing some of the
structures I will come to rely on later, including some early pop
culture criticism—

"Bad Medicine" is on. Oh, great. I just love Jon Bon
Jovi. And they have such original lyrics! I mean who
else would think of

Your love is like Bad medicine

(What is that like?)

Bad Medicine is what I need.

(DOES HE LIKE TO TAKE MEDICINE?)

OOOO, Shake it up, Bad Medicine

(Instructions!)

There Ain't No Doctor that

(Beautiful English. Double Negative.)

can cure my disease.

(What did he catch? And why would he take bad
medicine for it????)

"Born to be my Baby." Another original song. It starts
off, "Na Na Na Na Na Na Na Na Na Na." *Oooh.* She
was born to be his baby. What, did he give birth to her
and then become her boyfriend? THAT'S AGAINST
THE LAW!

On page sixty-four I break down the lyrics to Metallica's "One"
and mock them with delight. Pages seventy-nine to eighty-two
I'm going through the channels on my television, just listing my

choices. Page ninety-two I am talking yet again about Edie Brickell & New Bohemians, and on page fifty-three there's a straight-up Rick Roll, as I end a joke with the lyrics to "Never Gonna Give You Up."

Then, about halfway through the note, I get real.

[*PAGE 93*]

Well, I'm almost halfway finished with this note. Unbelievable. I'm going to have to tell you a long story to waste pages. Hmmmmmmmmmmm. Um-mmmmmmmmmmmmmmmm.

I don't want to tell you a big sob story.

Did you know I almost met Michael J. Fox? See, my mom worked with this guy from Canada who's sister went to school with MJF. ANYWAY, he was going to come to Palm Springs, and my mom's friend was going to show him around. So, I was going to meet Michael J. Fox. BUT (yes, there's always a depressing but to my stories) Michael J. Fox changed his mind to do a movie. You know, if Michael J. Fox decided to come to Palm Springs instead of doing a movie, we, to this day, would never of heard of BACK TO THE FUTURE.

Well, I guess it was a good excuse not to come to Palm Springs.

Have you ever tried to run away? I did. My family was having a few problems and I had my own problems (I never told my mom about what had happened. I've never told anyone, in fact. So don't take it personally if I don't tell you, I just don't want to tell anyone what happened to me.)

Those words are written in erasable pen, and you can see underneath I had originally written something else entirely.

Anyway, so I was 10 years old, and I packed my clothes, roller skates, shoes, pillow, and stuffed animal in my bag, left my house, and walked to my friend's house. I was there for 2 hours. My friend asked me (THIS IS A REALLY STUPID STORY) why I brought a bunch of things over and I told her I wanted to spend the night. So I did and I went home the next day.

GIVE ME A BREAK, I WAS TEN YEARS OLD!!! I WAS JUST A STUPID, SCARED KID!! I WAS CONFUSED, SO DON'T LAUGH AT ME! I WAS HUNGRY, SO I WENT HOME!!

"Never Tear Us Apart" is on TV. This is my favorite INXS song.

Now "My Perogative" is on. What the hell is a perogative? I'll look it up in the dictionary.

Well, it's not in this one. But this dictionary doesn't have many words. I'll look in another one.

It's not in this one either. Let me look for, yet another, dictionary.

I can't—wait—it's not in this one either. The song ended 10 minutes ago and I'm looking for a dictionary.

HE MADE THE WORD UP—ALRIGHT! THERE'S NO SUCH THING AS A PEROGATIVE! ONE MORE PAGE AND I'LL BE HALFWAY FINISHED!

I FINISHED HALF OF YOUR PRESENT! YEAH!

I have to clean the house. I'll write later.

I eventually tell Holly Hunter Boy the story of what happened to me. I told him the time he came to visit me for those short summer days when we watched those movies and I wished for him to understand how important he was to me. We were flipping through photo albums, looking at baby pictures of me, when I flinched at a photo I didn't know was included in the album of someone whose face I never wanted to see again.

Later that night, either Holly Hunter Boy asked or I decided to tell him my secret. When I finished, he asked to see the photo album again. He turned to the page where I flinched, peeled back the cellophane from the sticky, yellow adhesive, and popped out the photo.

"Tear it up," he said.

"I can't just do that. It's my mom's photo album."

"Tear it up right now."

I did, and then he held out his hand. "I'm taking these pieces back with me and I will throw them away far away from you. It's gone. It's all in your past and gone now."

As much as I may have teased Holly Hunter Boy for being an emotionally immature teenager during the time I hooked all my hopes and dreams on him, this story right here is how I know I wasn't wrong to love him.

Back to the note.

Sensing it's time for some levity, on pages 124-134 I briefly mention that I'm watching *National Lampoon's Vacation* before launching into a story about my antics at the mall that result in me coming home with only seventeen cents. A few pages later I have taped a dime, a nickel and two pennies.

I write a lot about *Saturday Night Live*, music, and just about lose my shit when I find out that Carrie read the notebook when I wasn't looking, which means she read the part where I was shit-talking her for taking one of my friends away. I spend many pages worried about whether or not she's going to kill me and breathlessly meld that with a story about my cat and then suddenly I'm all:

If McDonald's salads are tossed fresh all day, what if you come in at night?

Mommy, mommy, why do I keep walking in circles?
Shut up, or I'll nail your other foot to the floor.

With each page closer to my final goal my handwriting and mental stability become more frenetic. Sometimes I write in spirals or squares, there are pages where I've written sideways, upside-down. As I realize I will finish within five days, that I will be done not by Christmas, but by the end of the weekend, I declare that I won't be able to wait weeks to hand this over to Holly Hunter Boy, but will instead hand it to him the next day at school.

I stay up late and finish. My triumphant last page reads:

[*page 200*]

Well, here it is. I've poured my heart out to you for a Christmas present. Now I want a hug. I have written you 200 pages. Now, after I move, I want you to look at this once in a while. This is my way of expressing my friendship.

Stay the same way you are. Remember, you can be the jock you want to be and still stay as smart as you are. Good luck in your future.

Well, I better go now.

♥ ya.

Pam Ribon

(That's going to be worth money when I become famous!)

On the very last page of the notebook, you shouldn't be even the slightest bit surprised to learn I've included:

pre·rog·a·tive (/pri•räg•tiv/)

n. an exclusive privilege, esp. one peculiar to a rank, class, etc.

I don't remember if the 200-page note was your idea or mine. Do you? And what did you think when you got it? Why did you keep it?

I'll bet it was born over the phone. The origins of the idea were probably yours but I egged you on for aforementioned feelings of special-ness. But you have it now. Read it. It probably says.

I remember it being a pretty big deal.

In the archaeology classes that I taught, one recurring theme was that it is not the stuff that is the most telling, but the stuff that it is found with. Therefore, the note was in a box with many of my best memories from that time period. There are some pictures, yearbooks, and school papers as might be expected, and all of my karate belts.

I hope this helps.

—[Holly Hunter Boy]

I Just Want to Scream Hello

About a year after the Thanksgiving vacation debacle with Super Mario Brothers Boy, I get a phone call from him. He is apologetic, but mostly he is incredulous, because he has been living somewhere in Tennessee, and has run into Apology Boy. I hear both of their voices over the phone, and it is both heartbreaking and reassuring. They aren't as gone as they feel. They are simply *over there.*

I don't ever see Apology Boy again, although his name comes up. There's Facebook, and the town I'm from is small. There are people from back then I can find and some I still can't, and others who would like to keep the past back where it was.

About a week before I move to Los Angeles, I get another call from Super Mario Brothers Boy, who had been living in Boston. "I'm moving," he says.

"Me too!" I tell him. "Where are you going?"

"Los Angeles. Where are you headed?"

He arrived one day before I did, and he's been forever right—we still know each other. We are still in each other's lives. Sometimes he dates my friends, and sometimes he is gone for long periods of time, but he always comes back around, just as he promised.

"I have been paying an absolutely horrendous karmic debt," he once told me. "Every time I struggle in a relationship, I feel like I'm still paying penance to the things that happened between us when we were younger."

He still claims he had no idea I was trying to get him to sleep with me that night in our dorm room. He also met Soft Hair's pretty girlfriend. "I couldn't be gay anymore around her, either," I believe was his explanation. "That girl is crazy good looking."

As I write this it is Super Mario Brothers Boy's birthday. I send him an email that ends with: "Am I making it up, or is it true you went into the Haunted Asylum with [Soft Hair]?"

He replied: "I was talking about that hospital recently and I'd forgotten who I went there with until your email. I'm surprised we left you alone in the car though. Seems like a bad idea."

This book has definitely brought up some issues I hadn't realized were still unresolved, and it has been difficult at times to go back into some of my mistakes and awkward attempts at romance, but then I get this moment like Super Mario Brothers Boy finally admitting that it was probably a bad idea to leave me outside at night in Downtown Houston and I finally get some much-needed validation.

Because I'm unable to stop myself from self-mortification, I email him the same questions I sent Holly Hunter Boy. I hit "send" and then sit back and wonder when, if ever, I'm going to learn.

His reply comes much sooner than I've ever expected from him.

All I ask is that you don't print my actual name. I love you, but I'm not proud of the shit I put you through as a teen. I was pretty lame. I'm happy to answer any question you ever have for me.

What is your earliest memory of me? Meaning, how and when did you first notice me?

This is hard to say because I don't remember the exact moment. I know it was on the school bus and I was 14 or 15. I believe we became involved in a group conversation and that's when we first met. I am pretty sure my initial reaction to you was that I thought you were funny and I'm sure I was attracted to you. I was riddled with hormones and under-developed social skills at the time, so there's really no telling.

How would you have defined our relationship in high school?

Uh…is this really going in a book? (thought with a smile on my face). I would define our relationship in high school as very good friends that powered through quite a bit of sexual awkwardness in about as good of form as one can hope to. We were strangely highly functioning dysfunctional kids.

At a certain point you had to know I "liked you" liked you. Did it hit you at once, dawn on you, or was it clear because I told you?

I think it was clear because of the attention you paid me, but I don't know that I ever had any clue as to how I was supposed to handle it or what I was supposed to do. I was awash in social and sexual dysfunction.

What did you think when you started getting all these notes from me?

I loved the notes. Mostly because they were so thoroughly interesting. But it was also nice to have the attention. I liked being liked and I think at some point it became like a personal badge of pride…an internal one of course.

Did you ever think of trying to let me down gently?

I wouldn't have known where to start and I don't think the idea of letting you down was something I thought about. I think I quite liked the undefined and undeclared nature of our relationship. I mean, if I knew then what I know now…let's just say things would have been a lot different. Not necessarily relationship wise, but I wouldn't have been so confused and sexually janky. Like the "if you keep doing that you're going to have to kiss me" moment… wtf was that? It would have been a win/win, but for some reason I ran for the hills. Who knows…I was not as bright as I gave myself credit for being.

[*If I remember correctly, he is talking about a moment where we were playing Super Mario Brothers and also exchanging back massages, and perhaps he was trying to get some side-boob massage action? I feel bad that I'm not completely sure of what this memory is, but I think it speaks to how differently we remember our order of events.*]

Do you remember the time you wrote Lauren R---'s name on your arm three hundred times in pen?

Ugh…no. Sounds like me though.

Do you remember what video games you played with me?

Of course I do. That was some of the highlights of my adolescence. Seeing as how you didn't ask me to expound on this I'll just leave it at that. I remember it well.

I don't remember if the 205-page note was your idea or mine. Do you? And what did you think when you got it?

I think it was a hundred page note, but I think you and I have disagreed about this before.

It started because you'd written both myself and another boy very long notes and I think the one you wrote him was longer than the one I had gotten…so I believe it was almost like a challenge. I remember the next day getting it and being blown away by it. It was wild. There was like best of lists in it and all kinds of random/ interesting shit. As for what I thought when I got it, I thought it was awesome and in turn thought you were awesome. It impressed me and flattered me all at the same time. I had it nailed to my wall for at least a year. I believe I lost it in a moment of teen drama when I took everything off my walls in my room as some form of protest to some perceived injustice my mom had put me through. Which is hilarious in it's own right because the woman was so freaking good to me…still is.

Why did you keep it?

I kept it because it was awesome as well as out of respect for the effort on your part.

Some clarification about some of our "moments":

We didn't just play video games sitting next to each other. We fooled around while we were playing Super Mario Brothers 3. I'm almost positive of this. I feel like we would do things to each other while we were taking our turn playing the game. I could be wrong about this, but I don't think I am.

I also remember fooling around in your bed and stopping so I could watch a Tribe Called Quest video that was playing on the TV. I'm not proud of that either, but at this point it's like, just put it on my karmic tab.

Okay…and now I will speak to Little Pam.

Dear LP,

I wish I could go back in time and tell you that you weren't alone in the confusion and muck that was adolescence in the 90s. In many ways John Hughes doomed us all to being overly sentimental and thoroughly deluded creatures that thought a solid music cue and a witty comment with properly timed delivery could make all of our dreams come true. Maybe it wasn't just John's fault. I'm sure the entirety of the 80s is somewhat to blame as well.

I feel like to properly explain why you went through everything you went through it's somewhat necessary to explain about what it is like being an adolescent male. For starters, you're not very bright. You constantly think about sex, but you have no idea what it is or what you're supposed to do. You have to be cool, you have to be tough, and you genuinely never have any idea what is really going on. By default you think that you're supposed to fuck everything in the world that is soft and pretty, but again you have no idea why. Now couple that with being raised in an environment with zero role models of what a "healthy" male/female romantic relationship looks like outside of an 80s movie and you'll begin to understand where the sleeping dry humping comes from.

Most young men are selfish and stupid and horny to a fault.

Teen life is shitty no matter where you are. The same insecurities and desires haunt almost all of us. In some creepy way I almost feel like we were sort of family. Not incestuous or anything, but from the same cloth. I feel like this is why our relationship has endured. I also should point out that I really, really like your husband. So much so that I felt weird about writing some of this stuff.

I wish I could go back and tell you just how amazing you're going to turn out and how spectacularly you're going to crush the odds. I feel like somewhere down in there you always knew that you would come out on top and that despite all the confusion, frustration, and the colossal parental road blocks that life dealt you... that you'd win out in the end. You're going to be an amazing mom and I can't wait to watch your kid take over the planet. With any luck she'll be the world's first lesbian president.

I'm sorry for a lot of it, but not all of it.

Love Always,
[SMB Boy]

How To Write To Boys

(some advice for my daughter, who is currently six months old)

1. **Keep It Brief.** At first. Find out if that boy gets you before you give him your all.

2. **Keep It Simple.** I cannot tell you how many boys I wasted mixtapes on. You don't have to show him your entire world in the first week.

3. **Keep it Equal.** If you don't find what he has to say interesting, then you aren't trying to be with him, you're trying to be with *somebody*. That's not fair to either of you.

4. **Go Outside.** You have to have a life if you want to share one with somebody. Don't put your whole world into someone else's hands, because one day they might not be there and you will be completely lost and alone.

5. **Girls Exist, Too.** It took me way too long to realize the importance of my friendships. I hope you know from the beginning how special it can be between two girls who want to do nothing more than giggle and goof off all night long. I promise right now to always keep your popcorn bowl full and the movie nights kick-ass. The stronger your friendships are, the better you

will be as a girlfriend, because you will be well-versed in how to love someone's heart first, body second.

6. **Make Sure He's Single.** Speaking of girls, if the boy you like has a girlfriend, don't try to become his best friend. You will never be happy in the friend zone, and other girls will hate you so hard it'll hurt.

7. **Make a Second Draft.** Don't give him your first thoughts. Don't hit *send* right away. Don't hand someone your raw emotions. Sit with it for a second. Sleep on it before you regret saying something you weren't ready to share.

8. **Keep Your First Draft.** Save it for yourself. Save it for your future children. Save it for when you're in your twenties and miserable in love so you can see you used to have hope. Save it to remember the time before someone broke your heart. But most importantly, save it to remind yourself later that no matter how hard your life might be, it'll never be harder, longer, or more painful than those years you spent surviving high school.

1 Jan 93, 1:35am

[NICE BOY]—

I lost your ring. I'm not sure where, I think while I was throwing leaves at K— and S—. That's where K— lost his (I'm wearing it now; he doesn't know it's gone yet). I wish I knew where your ring was, I miss it. My finger feels naked. I feel naked. I remember at first I resented that ring because your mother picked it out. Now I'm ready to cry from staring at this tan line on my finger.

The tan line I got from your swimming pool...

I threw away my Far Side calender [*sic*]. I ripped off the last sheet and threw it away. It's hard to believe that a whole year passed already. I took down my other calender and made the mistake of looking through it. Those jotted notes hold more memories than most of my poems.

S's Christmas Party...Christmas Vacation with N—... Port LaVaca...Auditions for "Running,"...Chess club reminders...Tons of birthdays.

And then there's you. The first mention of you is something like "Study with—." Then "—leaves." "—comes home."...New Year's Eve...Gifted and Talented project. Then there's a green slash on February seventh. Laser Light Show…(28-29)

I will never regret falling in love with you. I wouldn't erase those times for anything.

I remember everything. Maybe even some things you don't. I remember "Shadows," the Aging Machine, our cartoons. "I'm seventeen." I remember our first night at the river with Doritos and Munch 'ems, where we hadn't discovered the kissing game yet. I remember the Digital Underground songs, the U2 songs, the Doors songs…even the Marky Mark videos.

I remember our secret monster-protecting forts, horror movies, touch therapy and *Dangerous Liaisons*. I remember how you taped [calculus teacher's] notes when I was ill, how we stayed on the phone till three. I remember sleeping in [English teacher's] class under a table with you. I remember sleeping in your arms in a bed in a hotel room and we <u>didn't do anything</u>. (We were such fools.) I remember getting lost on Main with you (several times).

I remember our bad times, too. Arguements [*sic*] over who said what to whom in what way. Worrying over who should call whom and how often. Worrying about my parents reaction to us.

I also remember the first day of summer (skinny dipping and pool tables and a $1000 bill). I remember studying logarythms. [*sic*] I remember our sex books and sex talks and phone sex. Our openness and frankness and honesty. I remember the opening night performance of *Rumors*, where we danced, and the festivities following the Friday night performance. I remember the library, *Basic Instinct*, and the countless videos we "watched" on lazy Sunday afternoons. I remember the box office in the theatre, the highway game, and our evenings at the river.

I remember our games, our tampon fights, and our war-ball matches. I remember the mirror of youth, holding your hand home from Bennihanas, and eating Death By Chocolate.

I won't forget how you held me when I was hurting. How you always knew how to make my heart pains go away and how to deal with my fears that kept me up at night. Maybe it really *was* a lawnmower.

I know that's what these things will remain…*memories*. I guess they're supposed to. I just wish that things didn't have to end or change or die. I would have loved to have kept that feeling forever.

I am seeing another now…I'm not sure if I'm doing the right thing. I know I like him and I don't want to hurt him, but at the same time I know that I am hurting me. I don't really know what to do. I don't see how or what he means when he tells me he loves me because I don't think that he really knows me yet. Plus, I'm scared. He makes me feel so little…

No matter who I'm with or holding it could never subtract the feelings we shared, or erase memories we formed. There will always be a place in my heart for Pseudoprom, Sadie Hawkins and Magic Island. There's a million sunsets stored there, dozens of roses, poems, songs, love letters, images of bodies outlined in moonlight, turtles, swans, Chinese food, and a brilliant foil rose.

I wish I could find your ring. I want to keep it to show my daughter someday. I want to pull out your drawing, your mum, your foil sculptures, your pictures and your stories and show the tangible side of true love, of first love, of real love...even if it doesn't live happily ever after.

1992 was a good year. I had the best friend that I've ever had. I had the strongest relationship I've ever seen. I fell in love deeper than ever before. Coincidence that they were all with the same person? Probably not.

I'll understand if you take down your posters or erase the messages from your mirror. That time is over. It is a memory. I do cry over it. People cry when beautiful things end. A part of me will always love you, [Nice Boy]. A big part. You will always be my turtle.

And yes, I do believe we'll meet again someday.

Love forever,
Pam

Acknowledgments

Julia Callahan loved, protected, and nurtured this book from start to finish. Thank you, Pesty, for all the support and guidance, and for making me feel like it mattered. Thanks to Tyson Cornell for asking me to do this in the first place. Special thanks to Alice Marsh-Elmer for her talent and grace under pressure.

As always, thanks to the team: Chad Christopher, Todd Christopher, Alexis Hurley, Alex Hertzberg, Greg Pedicin, and Brandy Rivers. Brandy was one of the first to really geek out about this book, and I love her for it.

Thanks to Cheri Nightingale and Avia Haynes, both of whom gave me the courage to revisit some darker times. Cayla Cardiff, Karina Whitacre, Glenda Lee and Amber Waskow got me through them when they happened. Thank you, wonderful ladies.

Dear boys in this book: some of you know about this, some of you don't, and some I hope never find out. Please try to consider all of this a compliment. (For most of you.)

Thank you to my family for their patience and love. It can't be easy living with me when I'm writing a book, so I appreciate how much you make it seem like this kind of behavior is all totally normal.

Elise Aliberti has quickly become my soul mate in every way I would have meant it at fourteen. Lady, I carry your heart in a giant bag that's got four bags in it and a few receipts and three spare buttons and a pacifier and some gum and thank you for all you do and I'm sorry I don't know more about Disney princesses.

Thank you to Kelly Eisert, Felicity Trevino, and Osnat Shurer, who for were there for that "I just wrote a first draft" moment. It's a big one, and I will always remember it.

Thanks to Courtney Upton for being my one-woman pro bono Gulf Coast publicity team. I enjoy watching your aggressive persuasion skills via Facebook.

Little Pam got her start with the fans of pamie.com, and I thank all of my readers for being such a warm, receptive audience. Thank you to Jessica Lasher for being so moved by my public ridiculousness that she created a Facebook fan page for Little Pam. And thanks to Sharon Long (who will always be Agata to me) for loving LP in such a pure, sweet way. I always knew you were laughing with her and laughing at me. Thank you for being so good at expressing the difference.

Thanks to the creators and audiences for the popular storytelling shows *True Tales of Lust and Love* and *Sunday Night Sex Talks* for reminding me how much I love to make people so very uncomfortable while they are laughing. And thanks to everyone who came out to a book signing and cringed their way through LP's awkwardica.

Special thanks to Liz Feldman dot org, who first suggested I read my giant letter to Homeroom Boy in front of strangers while she gleefully mocked me in the background. I'm so proud of what you've accomplished since we stepped off that stage.

And finally: Glark, if you are reading this right now PUT THE BOOK DOWN.